Pieces *of the* Puzzle

Pieces *of the* Puzzle

A Personal Journey
of Raising a Child With Special Needs

Wendy Keyes Roback

outskirtspress
DENVER, COLORADO

Pieces of the Puzzle
A Personal Journey of Raising a Child With Special Needs
All Rights Reserved.
Copyright © 2015 Wendy Keyes Roback
v1.0

Cover Photo © 2015 Wendy Keyes Roback. All rights reserved - used with permission.

Outskirts Press, Inc.
http://www.outskirtspress.com

ISBN: 978-1-4787-4290-6

Library of Congress Control Number: 2014918310

Outskirts Press and the "OP" logo are trademarks belonging to Outskirts Press, Inc.

PRINTED IN THE UNITED STATES OF AMERICA

Chapter 1

"Isn't it hard?" she asked. The question was well-intentioned and innocently posed, and yet I found myself taking offense to it. The meaning behind the question was "Isn't it hard raising a special needs child?" This was during the time before so many of the mysteries of my son, Jaden, had been unlocked, and I found myself thinking, *You want me to say it's hard to be a parent to my child? Who says that? What kind of parent would I be if I said yes? Of course it's not hard. It's my job. It's what I signed up for the day he was born.* I, however, did not reply with any of those comments. To be honest, I don't remember my reply, but I'm sure I mumbled something to the effect of "It has its moments," or "Sometimes." Whatever my reply may have been, I know it was something short and sweet. I'm not sure why this exchange sticks out in my mind, but it does. It is one of those moments that I've replayed in my head many times over, and if I could have a "do-over," my reply would be much more detailed and eloquent than whatever words I managed to eke out when first asked that question

One answer to the question "Isn't it hard?" is this: Hard compared to what? You see, Jaden is my first and only child, so I have no frame of reference to compare him to. Sure, I have James and Jen, my stepchildren, and yes I've been around them since they were just little kids, but truth be told, they have a mom and they have a dad, and I play neither of those roles—their parents do that just fine. The day-to-day tasks of running a sick kid to the doctor or for a well-child checkup, carting a kid to and from after-school activities, and all of the other fun things parents get to do falls to them and not me. Sure, if and when needed I'm there as a fill-in, but I am not their parent. I am someone who loves them unconditionally, someone they can come to, talk to, someone who's there for them, but I am not their mom.

So again I ask, hard compared to what? I know not everyone believes in a higher power, but I do, and I think God knew just what he was doing when he planned on giving me Jaden. I can't say that it's hard because I have nothing to compare it to. Oh sure, there are moments that are hard, just as there are moments that are easy, but isn't that true for all parents, whether their children are special needs or not?

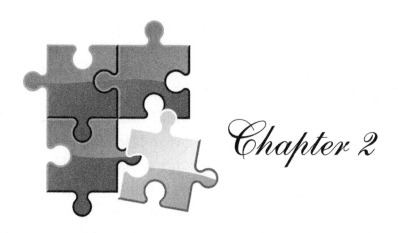

Chapter 2

I've heard that all good books start at the beginning, so I guess now would be a good time for me to back up and start at the beginning. My name is Wendy Roback, and though this book will have several star players, the MVP of this book is my son, Jaden. It's a look into the world of what it's been like to raise this unique child, the high highs, the low lows, and everything in between.

My husband, Glenn, and I had been together for several years before Jaden was conceived, however we weren't married, or even engaged for that matter, so people naturally assumed Jaden was an "oops." That, however, couldn't be further from the truth. Yep, Glenn and I did things backward by most standards. We got engaged and then married all while I was pregnant, talk about a whirlwind. But Jaden really was planned for, prayed for, and wanted very much.

Glenn and I had actually tried for quite some time to get pregnant before it happened. It was 2006; I was in my early twenties, Glenn in his early forties. One day I sat down and wrote a letter to God, asking—no, actually more like begging—for a child and promising to be the best mom I could be if only I could have a child. Very shortly after that, Jaden was conceived. I often think of myself as quirky and dorky and thought the same of my letter, so I didn't save it. Looking back I wish I had saved that. It would have been neat to have had it to give to Jaden someday. It was only a few months after my grandfather passed away that I became pregnant, and part of me wonders if he had a helping hand in the matter, at least that's what I like to think. Though several J-names were in the running, Jaden was what Glenn and I settled on, and it is a perfect fit: the name Jaden (spelled Jadon in the Old Testament) means "God has heard." God had heard my prayers for a child, and I was blessed with Jaden.

Getting pregnant was hard, but telling my parents, well, that was even harder. Long story short, my parents couldn't stand Glenn. Glenn and I had been together for four years. Glenn had two children, James and Jennifer, from a previous marriage. Glenn is 20 years older than I and my parents felt that Glenn had stolen their baby girl, and they resented him for it. My mom was devastated when I broke the news. My father, the ever so calm one, reassured me it would take time but that my mom would come around. It's funny how a child changes everything; my father was right, and as time went on, my mom eventually did indeed come around. Jaden arrived, and today Glenn and my mom get along pretty well.

My pregnancy itself was pretty easy. There were however a few scares during the experience. A routine blood test came back abnormal, so it was recommended that I have an amniocentesis preformed. It was two weeks of worrying—will everything be okay?—and jumping every time the phone rang. Finally we got the results and learned that all was well.

But Jaden wasn't as active in the womb as a lot of babies are. I'd lie on my bed every night doing kick counts. You needed to feel the baby move a certain number of times in an hour and we didn't always hit the magic number. In hindsight I think I know why; we'll get to that later. For now I'll just say that Jaden was pretty chill in the womb and stayed much the same after birth.

Chapter 3

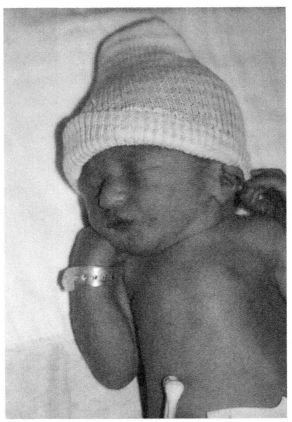

Jaden Alexander Roback

It was a cold February morning, two weeks before my due date. I left work for my last scheduled prenatal appointment. It was to be a run-of-the-mill day. I was just going to have a sonogram to get a measurement of approximately how big the baby would be when he was born. Glenn didn't come to this appointment because both James and Jennifer were home from school. It was midwinter break, and Glenn and the kids were going to be headed out for a day of sledding, while I was supposed to go back to work after my appointment.

I remember going into the sonogram room, and I recall how the technician suddenly got quiet, and then asked if I had been leaking any fluids. The answer was no. She asked how I felt about having the baby that day. Thoughts began to swirl in my head. *What do you mean have the baby today? My bag is not packed. I have work. The baby room isn't even done yet. Are you nuts?* The technician left the room to go speak with the doctor and then sent me upstairs to see him. I called Glenn from the waiting room and told him what was happening and the news that I anticipated the doctor might soon be giving to me. Another woman in the waiting room was staring at me and smiling as she heard my conversation with Glenn; it was a congratulations smile. But in my head I was thinking, *This can't be happening, not today anyway.* I wasn't the only upset one; Jennifer was upset, too. I was likely going to ruin her sledding day.

After my ob-gyn, called me into his office, he began, "First I need you to know that the baby is okay, but you need to go to the hospital now. Your amniotic fluid has disappeared and it's not safe for the baby. We need to get him out. Wendy, I know you. Do not go back to work. Do not go home to get your bag. You need to go straight to the hospital. I know how long it takes to get there; the on call physician will be expecting your arrival." Though based on what the sonogram technician had said to me this was pretty much the news I was expecting to hear, it was surely not the news I *wanted* to hear.

I started to drive toward the hospital and then, in tears, pulled the car over. I couldn't go to the hospital yet: people needed to know. I had to call work, as they were expecting me back any minute. I had to call Glenn again and also my parents to tell them the news.

I made my phone calls, pulled myself together, and continued on my way, arriving a few minutes later at the hospital. As I was told there would be, a doctor was there waiting for me. It was explained that given the circumstances it would not safe to have a vaginal delivery and that I would need a C-section. It was not an emergency C-section, but things went quickly. I was hooked up to IVs as they waited for Glenn and my parents to arrive, and once they did Glenn was suited up in a funny blue surgical gown and I was wheeled away. That day was one of the very first times I can recall my mom being nice to Glenn. She actually helped tie the back of his surgical suit and said congratulations to him. As I said, it's funny how a child changes everything.

At 3:06 p.m. on February 20, 2007, Jaden Alexander Roback came into the world. He was five pounds three ounces, and eighteen and a half inches long. Because of a spot—or what is called a skin dimple—on Jaden's back, the doctors ordered an X-ray of his spine, but the results revealed no spinal defects. Jaden was healthy, beautiful, and perfect. And I was terrified of him. *What was I thinking? What did I get myself into? What if I break him?* Glenn left late that evening, exhausted from the events of the day, and he still had to go home and finish the nursery. My parents and younger brother Dillon stayed until the nurse came in and said it was time for visitors to leave. I almost cried, and with my voice cracking as I looked at my mom, I told the nurse, "No, she can't leave! She can't leave until she changes his diaper." I was emotional from the day and was on the verge of tears again. I was afraid—no, actually I think a better word is *petrified*—to change my own child's diaper! Jaden and I have come such a very long way since that night.

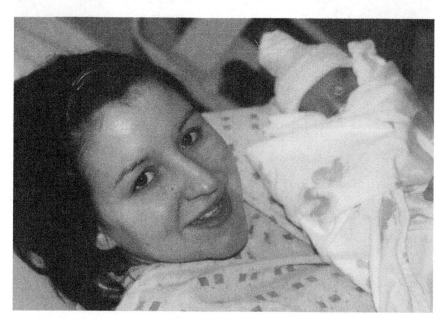

Holding Jaden . the first time

Glenn, James, Jennifer and Jaden

Chapter 4

The day Jaden and I were discharged from the hospital, I was told that he had failed his newborn hearing screening and that I needed to bring him to our local hospital in two weeks for a follow-up. They said, "It's nothing to worry about; it's pretty common for a child to fail their hearing test at birth. Usually the child ends up hearing just fine." Two weeks later Glenn and I showed up for Jaden's hearing test and were happy to get the news that the nurse who had reassured us was right: Jaden's hearing was fine.

The next several months went by without incident. Jaden was a happy baby. He was quiet and mellow, just as he had been in the womb. He was content to be held and snuggled all day long, and that was just fine with me, too. I loved to hold and snuggle him. It did take what seemed like forever for Jaden to sleep through the night—he was about eight or nine months old before he finally did that—but otherwise he was by all accounts an easy baby. To be honest, I couldn't complain about Jaden's waking up at night as an infant. Glenn and I have always worked opposite shifts, and he was usually just getting home and was still awake when Jaden awoke, so more often than not he handled the late-night feeding and I was able to sleep.

Being a first-time mom, I of course had the book that is often the go-to book for newbie moms, *What to Expect the First Year*. Jaden was meeting his milestones, though he was always on the later end of normal. He was six months old and not sitting up yet; he was nine months old and he was almost sitting up but still a bit floppy. Also he wasn't really babbling yet and was nowhere close to crawling.

It was at his one-year checkup that I brought up my concerns to Jaden's awesome pediatrician, Dawn Bard, M.D. She reassured me of what I already knew: he was still within the normal range of development, but was at the latter end of it. We discussed how early intervention (EI) services might help a child like Jaden in his development and growth, but decided to wait a bit before moving forward with EI.

Chapter 5

Before the fall

March 24, 2008, was the first time my ego as a mom was crushed. Glenn was at work and I was playing photographer. It was early evening, and thirteen-month-old Jaden was sitting on our bed and I was taking pictures of him. I had him stripped down to a diaper, and at first I had posed him with just a tie around his neck, then with only a winter hat on his head. I was having fun posing Jaden, taking what I thought were some really cute photos. I don't remember why or for what reason, but I turned around for a second, and just as I was turning, there was Jaden falling headfirst off the bed and onto the floor with a loud thud followed by tears. Glenn was at work and I called him in a panic and told him we had to go to the ER.

I expected him to be angry with me, and I'm sure he was, but he didn't say anything. He didn't need to. I was angry enough with myself. At the ER, the nurse could read me like a book. "Mom," she said, "he'll be just fine, and so will you." Cue the tears and hyperventilation, as in between sobs I said, *"But . . . what . . . if . . . he's . . . not?"*

Given the late hour, Jaden was hungry, tired, and cranky. He wanted juice and we couldn't give him anything until we got the all-clear from the doctor. What seemed like hours went by before the doctor finally came in and told us to sit down, and we knew immediately that something was wrong. "The CAT scan shows that your son has a mass near his brain. He'll need to see his pediatrician tomorrow, and he'll also need an MRI and likely neurosurgeons consult."

The questions started spilling from my mouth as quickly as I could form the words. "All this from a fall? Did I give him brain damage by letting him fall? What kind of mass? Neurosurgeon? You mean a brain surgeon? What is going on?"

The doctor assured me that although he didn't have all of the answers, he knew that Jaden had not been injured in the fall. The mass—this thing inside of my baby's head, whatever it was—had nothing at all to do with the fall. The doctor told us we should look at the fall as a blessing in disguise, because now we know about "it." His words were of very little comfort; we left the ER more worried than when we had come in. I cried myself to sleep that night, for not only had I let Jaden fall on my watch, but now there was possibly something very seriously wrong with him.

On March 28, four days after his fall, Jaden had an MRI. On April 15, we had the follow-up consultation with a neurosurgeon in Syracuse, New York, which is about an hour away from our home. We were told, "Jaden has an arachnoid cyst. It hopefully should never cause any issues, and surgery is more risky than leaving it alone. He'll need a follow-up MRI in nine months."

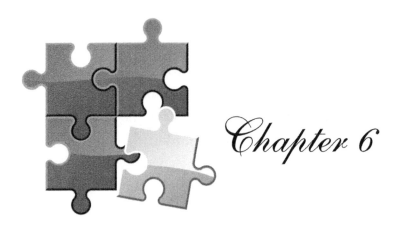

Chapter 6

In June I decided to proceed with early intervention and scheduled Jaden's evaluation for the following month. At the full evaluation in July, it was determined that he could benefit from basic skills, speech, and physical therapies. Not everyone thought Jaden needed EI services or that we needed to look into them, but I did. I didn't even know if Glenn was 100 percent on board at the time, but he let me follow through with it and never once voiced any complaints. I do, however, vividly remember at a family gathering around that time the possibility of us looking into EI was brought up and my brother-in-law, Bob, with the best of intentions, let me know his thoughts on the topic. "He [Jaden] doesn't need therapy. All he needs is to play and to be a boy."

Yes, Bob meant well, but he was also very vocal on the topic as was his nature on most topics, and he went on and on until his wife, Carol, told him to put a sock in it. I don't remember exactly what I said, but I do remember it being something to the effect of "Well, it's not gonna hurt anything! If you have a problem with something that I am doing with Jaden that might actually harm him, then as his uncle and godfather by all means tell me, yell at me, and voice your concerns to me. But if it's not going to hurt him, then I don't want to hear it." One of my best friends, Kristen, said I looked as if I wanted to jump over the table and strangle Bob. Looking back, EI was one of the best things we could have done for Jaden. Even if it didn't end up helping him (which it did), we understood for certain that it couldn't possibly hurt him.

Chapter 7

All too soon Jaden's therapies began, and our home became a revolving door of therapists coming in and out of the house. Jaden started with basic skills and physical therapy twice per week and speech therapy three times per week. Lisa did basic skills, Lauren did speech therapy, and Mike did physical therapy. Jaden was pretty good for Lisa; he enjoyed most of the puzzles and toys she brought for him to play with, and he worked really hard and well for her. For Lauren it would depend on the day. Some days Jaden would sit on his hands and close his eyes, wanting nothing to do with Lauren or what she wanted to work on, and other days he was a happy camper and loved every minute of his time with her. Ah, but Mike, that poor man had to have thick skin because working with my son would have given me a complex if I were him. Jaden would start crying every single time Mike walked in the door. He would crawl under the coffee table and Mike would have to physically pull him out. And when it was time for Mike to leave, Jaden knew it and would happily help Mike pack up the toys, hug him good-bye, and most days he would also crawl to the kitchen to wave good-bye as the door closed behind the therapist. This went on from the first day Mike worked with Jaden until the very last. Mike would come, Jaden would cry, Mike would leave, and Jaden would all too eagerly wave good-bye at him.

Glenn never once complained about EI, but even if he had, I wouldn't have blamed him, as it was his days that were impacted, not mine. As Jaden's mom, I of course wanted to know what I needed to be working on and doing at home, and so I tried to be there for as many therapy sessions as possible. But more often than not, Jaden's appointments were during the day when I was at work. I was lucky to catch the beginning or end of a session; occasionally, I would catch the middle of a session if one happened to be going on when I came home for lunch. Glenn was the one who was home with Jaden during the day, and so it was he who had to schedule naps, appointments, trips to the store, and any other daily activities around Jaden's therapy sessions.

Jaden working hard during physical therapy with Mike

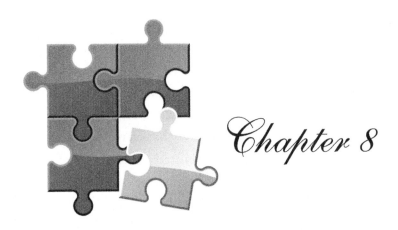

Chapter 8

The nine months since the March MRI that identified Jaden's cyst came and went, and the follow-up MRI in December showed that it hadn't gotten any bigger, so we were told that the cyst probably never would get bigger, and no further follow-ups were needed unless issues should arise. We were advised to be on the lookout for seizures and migraines as Jaden got older, and if problems such as those came up, the doctors would need to check on the cyst again.

To this day I wish they could just remove it. Every time Jaden has a headache, I worry about it. Anytime I suspect my son is acting the least bit unusual, I worry about it. Had the cyst been removed, there would be one less thing in the back of my mind to be constantly worried about.

Jaden was making a lot of progress in EI, but he was still delayed. I didn't know what, but I knew something just wasn't right. He had feeding issues, he was very wobbly on his feet, and his speech . . . what about his speech? I just wanted to hear *Mama*, that's all. We had this awesome speech therapist, and I often wondered why Jaden wouldn't talk for her. *He's smart, but odd. Is he autistic? I thought autistic children weren't affectionate, and he's so very loving. What is wrong with this child?* Those were the kinds of thoughts that so very often flooded my head.

When I feel comfortable with someone, I'm—as my older brother, Mike, says—rather blunt. My bluntness applies to myself, my child, my family, and anyone and everyone; that is, anyone and everyone who I feel comfortable with.

I remember voicing concerns to both Mike and my mother that there was something off; that something was not right. In particular I remember a conversation with Mike in which I was being quite honest. I don't remember exactly what I said but it was something to the effect of "There is something wrong with this child. There is! I don't know what it is, but he's not normal." I do believe my tone was rather harsh. Mike thought I was being brutal, and we got into a screaming match over the phone where Mike told me, "There's nothing wrong with him! Jaden's a normal little kid!" And I was yelling back, "No! No, he's not!" The call ended with me hanging up on Mike.

Chapter 9

Since Jaden still wasn't talking, or really even babbling, he underwent four hearing tests between his first and second birthdays. Scribbled across the outcome line on each report for these tests was "CNT" (Could Not Test). Each time I was assured, "We think he can hear; he's just not cooperative today. If he's not doing this or that in X number of months, come back." Jaden's speech therapist was pretty confident he could hear, and depending on the day, I thought he could, too.

I wish I had been more educated on the topic at the time. I trusted the audiologists we were seeing. Had it been the me of today, "CNT" would not have flown with this mama.

It wasn't until years later that I watched the movie *Mr. Holland's Opus*, where there is a scene when the mom drops pans behind her child and he doesn't startle or react in any way. She discovers then that her child is deaf. As I watched, tears were rolling down my cheeks, as it took me back to this time, to a place where I vividly remember doing the same exact thing, and I, too, received no response from my child.

The same week that I dropped pans behind Jaden, I also remember vacuuming the living room floor and he turned around and growled at me because I was interrupting the TV show he was watching. He could hear. I knew then that I was worrying for nothing. Jaden could hear. I called Glenn, my mom, and my sister-in-law, Carol, to tell all of them that this kid hears just fine. He still wasn't talking, though, but if he can hear, then what's the real issue?

It was at the hearing test Jaden had just before he turned two, in early 2009, that I heard it again: "We think he can hear." Then the audiologist started to say, "If he's not babbling by . . ." By now, my blood was boiling. It was the first and only time I have ever yelled at a medical professional who was trying to help my child. I rudely cut her off and said, "No! You listen. I want to know if he can hear or if he can't! I want to help him, and I can't do that without an answer! So, you listen. You need to give me an answer!" It was then that I heard "Well, there is this test we can do. It's called an ABR, and it will give us an answer. Why don't you come back in a few weeks and we'll perform the test." I scheduled the appointment without saying anything further, but I was thinking to myself, *Wait . . . there has been this test that you could have done long, long ago that you're just now telling me about? You wait until I am in tears, until I have reached my breaking point and have rudely yelled at you, to offer this test to me!* Livid. I was livid.

Chapter 10

March 2, 2009. The second time my mom ego was crushed.

It was the scheduled date of Jaden's ABR test. His speech therapist, Lauren, had tried to reassure us that she thought the test would come out fine. She didn't have the answers to why Jaden wasn't speaking, but she did think he could hear. We were told the test would take about two hours, and that Jaden would have to be very quiet and still. You try keeping a two-year-old quiet and still for two hours. This would *not* be fun.

As the specialists had been telling us for over a year now that they thought Jaden could hear, we were expecting to learn more of the same. Only one of us could be in the room during the test, and because of that, we decided Glenn would stay home and just Jaden and I would go.

ABR stands for auditory brain response. I am not good with technical descriptions, and so my very basic layperson's understanding of the test is that it is used to measure the brain's response to noise stimulation. To receive and relay the response that Jaden's brain would have to that stimulation, little electrodes were placed all over his head. With this test, we would know once and for all if his brain was or was not responding to noise.

Jaden did squirm around some during the experience, but overall he was pretty good. The test was completed, and we were sent back to the waiting room. I was in a chair with Jaden on my lap, in a room full of other patients, when the same person who did Jaden's repeat neonatal hearing evaluation when he was two weeks of age, the same person who back then told me Jaden could hear fine, the same person who also did some of Jaden's subsequent tests, was now telling me that my child was deaf.

"Mrs. Roback, I don't know what happened. I myself performed the test at two weeks, and so I know it was accurate. We know for certain today that Jaden has a severe to profound hearing loss in his right ear and a moderate one in his left ear. Would you like to proceed with amplification? Would you like us to get in touch with a deaf infant teacher on your behalf?"

My head was spinning at a thousand miles a minute. I must have sounded so clueless to those also in the waiting room, hearing our conversation as I asked, "Amplification?"

"Yes, hearing aids," was the reply.

I didn't even know what to think, but I answered with "Yes, if that's what he needs" Hearing aids were ordered that day.

I had taken just the half day off from work and was already running late. I didn't break the news to Glenn in the nicest of ways, and if I could have a do-over, Glenn would have been told in a much better manner.

I remember that I carried Jaden up the stairs and into the house—he was just really starting to walk and still wobbly on his feet, so we carried him up and down stairs. Glenn was in the computer room, and I sat Jaden down next to Glenn and said, "He's deaf. I gotta go."

Naturally his reply was "What do you mean he's deaf?"

"Just what I said. They said he's deaf, they ordered hearing aids, and I gotta go. I am late to work." I kissed Jaden on the head and left. That surely wasn't the best way to tell parent-news to a spouse, but it was how I told Glenn.

I was overwhelmed. I was mad at myself. I shed more than a few tears that day. *How could I not know my child was deaf! What type of mother am I! Who has a deaf kid and doesn't know it!* All of the books I'd been reading to him for years he couldn't even hear. No wonder why the boy can't talk. No wonder why he's delayed! He's missed out on a solid two years of crucial and important learning time. He's missed out on a time when stimulation to a child is of the upmost importance and I, his mother, had been clueless about this problem.

I was never upset about Jaden being deaf or hard of hearing. On the contrary, I was upset and felt much animosity toward myself for not having known. I was upset for the time that he had missed out on hearing. I felt an indescribable guilt that I may always feel. Had Jaden been diagnosed when born he would have had the benefit of using hearing aids from birth forward, this would have greatly benefited his speech and language development.

Yes, I was upset with myself, but I was even more upset with the audiologist who claimed she did the test correctly when Jaden was two weeks old. If I could have had the kind of meltdown that is common among toddlers, I would have screamed at her, "Liar, liar pants on fire! Do not feed me some crop of crap telling me you did your job correctly. No, you didn't. You failed my child.

There is no excuse. This should have been picked up on years ago." My worst fears had been vindicated. I felt like screaming to everyone and no one, all at the same time, "See, you little jerks, I told you there was a problem! I told you something wasn't right. Now let's fix it!" I did realize that my child was fine the way he is, that he's not broken and doesn't need fixing, but I still longed to hear him speak words like *Mama*. If hearing aids were the key to communicating with him and helping him communicate with us, then I wanted him to have them.

Shortly after Jaden's diagnosis, we met Joan; she would become Jaden's deaf infant teacher. Joan would tell me that I had nothing to feel bad about. She would explain that it's hard when the child does not have a total hearing loss. The child may laugh at the barking sound of a dog, as Jaden so often did, and therefore you think the child can hear. The child may smile when you talk to him, and you think he can hear you, but really he is just smiling at the sight of his mama rather than at what is being said. The child is hearing bits and pieces of the world around him but is not getting the whole story, and you are given mixed signals. Can he or can't he hear? Joan would tell me many times how it becomes much trickier to connect the dots with the child who has some hearing. The logical part of my brain knows that Joan is right and everything she says is true. These are things that I myself would now tell any other parent in my shoes, and yet a part of me considers my lack of foresight as a "mom fail."

Jaden shortly after getting his first hearing aids

Everyone was surprised by the news of Jaden's hearing problems, but it was full steam ahead. In hindsight, it was no wonder Jaden had been so chill in the womb and such a chill baby. While most babies are hearing their mother's voice while in the womb, Jaden may not have heard my singing "I Love You" lullabies to him. While most babies start babbling in response to hearing Mom, Dad, and everyone else around them talking to them, Jaden heard little or none of that. It all makes sense now. I'd be chill, too, if the world around me was quiet.

Lauren and Jaden had already been working on signs, and now they would intensify their work on signs. Jaden was fitted with his hearing aids in April. His work with Lisa in basic skills and Mike in physical therapy was also continuing, and now Joan had been added to our team. I remember our first time meeting her. Jaden was quite ill with pneumonia so Joan couldn't work with him at all, so instead she worked with Glenn and me. She explained an audiogram to us in depth, and we learned all about something called a speech banana. We discussed the different options we have for communication and many more items that I would soon become all too familiar with. Joan was a godsend, a source of knowledge and information to our family when we were thrust into this new and unfamiliar world of having a deaf or hard of hearing child.

As our family dealt with the hectic process of dealing with Jaden's hearing loss, he also had another EI evaluation around this time, where it was determined he could benefit from occupational therapy, or the therapeutic use of basic everyday activities. Soon, Anne would join the team as his occupational therapist.

The hearing loss did not explain all of Jaden's issues. I still didn't know why Jaden had such low muscle tone and weak fine and gross motor skills, but at least I knew why he wasn't talking. I looked at our newfound knowledge as a blessing. A piece of the puzzle that is Jaden had been put together. Mike and Anne would work on gross and fine motor skills twice a week, and Lisa would continue working on basic skills, also twice a week. With the help of Lauren and now Joan, our family could begin to really address Jaden's communication issues. Jaden started picking up signs, especially for his favorite things like milk and cookies, more quickly than I could keep up with, and he was finally babbling now and even had a handful of words under his belt.

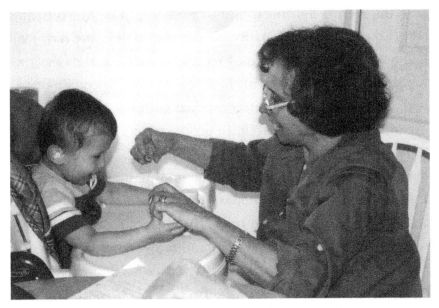

Joan and Jaden working together during a session

Chapter 12

I've never considered Jaden special needs, but in terms of the services he needs he is a special needs child. Dealing with EI and later school, one thing a parent will quickly learn is that goals are set far in advance and things move quickly. You may find yourself in a meeting discussing goals for the next six months, though you have trouble even envisioning what your child will or won't be able to do tomorrow. Jaden was two and a half now, and it was time to start discussing transitioning.

When I first heard that word in context of my child, I thought, *Transitioning? Where? To what? School? He's not even three yet. This is crazy!* But we needed to have a plan in place. Based on Jaden's birth date, our options were that he could stay in EI until June 30, 2010, or he could go to pre-K in January 2010. And so began the debate of whether to transition Jaden to pre-K or to keep him in early intervention.

Luckily for us, we had Joan in our corner. It happened that Joan worked for the New York State School for the Deaf (NYSSD), located in Rome, New York, which is about a thirty-minute drive from where we live. Joan told us about a program there called Little Listeners. Its focus is on language, speech acquisition, and getting children to use the hearing they do have for listening skills. The kids use sign as well as speech, with teachers speaking and reinforcing with sign as is needed. Some kids use sign more than speech; others use speech more than sign. Each individual child gets whatever he or she needs at any particular time. Joan couldn't say enough positive things about Cathy Lee, the pre-K teacher at NYSSD, and the team who worked with her.

It was late October 2009. A hectic time, as the holidays were approaching. Glenn and I had decided to expand our family and were trying for another child. Sure, Jaden had issues and we didn't have all of the answers, but we were handling it, and—not to sound cocky—I thought we were doing a darn good job of it, too. We didn't know what the future would hold for Jaden, but we could handle it, so now was the time to add another child to the mix.

We soon had to make a decision about Jaden, and whether we were going to enter Jaden in pre-K or keep him in EI, It was time to do our due diligence and pay a visit to the place we were considering. Glenn and I would soon go to visit NYSSD.

We'd never been to the school, so Joan accompanied us. We met Cathy Lee and her classroom assistant at the time, Nancy Lopus. We met the speech therapist who works with the kids in the program, Gail Ashmore, and also the school audiologist, Kim Sacco. It was nothing too formal, just your basic hi and how are you's. Then we got to observe. Observing the class was pretty neat. The classroom has an observation room, so we were able to watch the kids from behind a one-way glass mirror; they had no clue we were there, so they were their natural selves. I fell in the love with the teacher and her class that day. It was a small class with a friendly teacher and the kids seemed happy, they liked where they were, they were having fun, they were learning, and they were even talking. I couldn't understand all of the children, but I could understand many of them. No wonder why Joan couldn't say enough positive things about this program or teacher.

In early November it was time for the school evaluation process. Jaden would come and meet the audiologist, the school psychologist, the teacher, and the speech therapist. They would observe him, and then he would also get to visit a class and interact with the kids in the class. Based on this visit, recommendations would be made as to whether Jaden was ready for pre-K or not. Though we didn't yet know what the evaluators' recommendations would be, we did know that if we were going to send Jaden to school in January—or even if not until September—we wanted him to go to NYSSD.

Because NYSSD is a state school, a phone interview with the state would be needed. At the conclusion of the phone interview, the woman conducting the interview said to me, "No decisions have been made at this time. Technically, Jaden hears too well to qualify to attend NYSSD. You should know that he may not be accepted into the program." To say that I freaked out was an understatement. As soon as I was off the phone with the state I called Joan in tears. "What do they mean they might not accept him? This is where I want him to go!" Joan was just as upset as I, but calmed me down and reassured me that Jaden would probably be accepted into the program after all.

In late November Glenn and I traveled back to NYSSD for a meeting to discuss the findings of the observation. It was our D-Day, as we would have to make our decision. Both Glenn and I knew where we wanted Jaden to go to school. The big debate in our house was when? We both loved our early intervention team, but I wanted Jaden to go to school in January. Jaden had had limited interaction with kids his age, the occasional visit to the park and that was about it. Jaden could surely benefit from additional social interaction, and he would continue to get all of his therapies at school. I also didn't want Jaden to go without therapy for the months of July and August, and if he went to school in January he could then also attend summer school and get therapy throughout the summer.

Glenn, on the other hand, didn't feel the same way as I. He thought Jaden was too young to go to school. Not to mention that Glenn was accustomed to having his little buddy home with him every day, just the two guys while mom was at work. If Jaden were to go to school, Glenn would see him much less because when Jaden was getting home from school Glenn would be leaving for work. He was heartbroken over the thought of not seeing Jaden as much in the future.

We met in a conference room and discussed the findings of the evaluation. Cathy Lee; the school psychologist, Cindy Killian; and the other evaluators let us know that Jaden was delayed in many areas; this was not news to us. Then we heard from the speech therapist, who let us know that day that she wasn't sure how much, if at all, Jaden's speech would improve until she worked with him. It was a reality neither Glenn nor I had truly thought of before. Since Jaden was babbling now, and even saying a few words, the next step would naturally be speech, or so we thought. We hadn't thought about the what-ifs, as in what if his speech doesn't improve even with the appropriate therapy? It was a real possibility, and it was a reality that we needed to be aware of. I am grateful for what the speech therapist told us that day.

At the table all eyes were on us, as the interviewers awaited our decision. I said, "I don't know. I rely on you guys as professionals to tell me, after working with him for a little while; do you think he's ready?" Glenn voiced his concerns. Finally, we were told, "Yes, he is little, but we think he's ready. We think he can handle it." That was all I needed to hear. Despite Glenn's concerns, the decision was made that day. In January we would send our not yet three-year-old on a bus to attend a full day of school about half an hour from home.

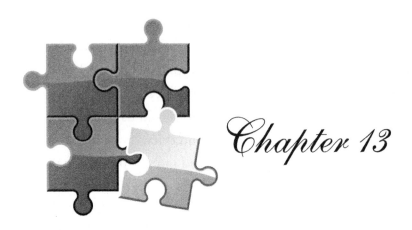

Chapter 13

Jaden had come so far in EI. With the help of Lisa, he was on point with his basic skills. He could color match, and knew how to play appropriately with toys. The only thing holding him back in that regard, were his weak communication skills. We had Lauren to thank that he was babbling and saying a few words. Granted, a lot of what he said wasn't pronounced correctly, and some of his words were just the basic animal sounds like *moo*, but he gained those skills under her guidance and care. With the help of Joan, he knew quite a few signs, and Mom and Dad were starting to feel more comfortable with this new world of having a hard of hearing child. Jaden still had a ways to go with fine motor skills, but he was making steady improvements with the help of Anne, and thanks to Mike Jaden was walking and even running, although a little wobbly when doing so. In late December 2010, it was time to say good-bye to his EI team. Jaden would start school in January, just after Christmas break.

January 4, 2010, was the day my husband and I were going to send our baby on bus to Rome to attend a full day of school five days a week. Most moms cry on their kids' first day of school. Not I. I tend not to be overly emotional when I'm "in it" and going through "it," whatever it may be. It's usually not until long after the fact that I get emotional. Even if I had wanted to cry, I wouldn't have. I was the one who wanted this. I couldn't be emotional over it!

The only thing I was upset about on the day Jaden was going off to school was that I was not able to go into work late that day, so I would miss seeing Jaden getting on the bus. It's just as well: the bus ending up being much later than we had been led to expect, and when Glenn decided the bus must have forgotten Jaden, he simply drove him to school that day. It was the bus ride that never was.

Waiting for the bus ride that never was

Though Jaden had made such progress in EI, the boy we sent off to school that freezing January day had a long, long way to go. His new team would be inheriting a child with issues that even we as his parents still didn't fully understand. Would his teachers be up for the challenge?

The Jaden we sent off to school was a sweet and loving child, but he was extremely shy, at times inappropriately so. He would oftentimes look down and cry if someone he didn't know tried to work with him or say hi to him. He would hide under tables when he felt uncomfortable, and he had sensory issues. Lord help the person who wanted him to get his hands dirty with something like finger paint, because a meltdown would surly ensue.

Jaden had feeding issues and ate mostly stage 3 baby food; if you tried to give him something he did not want, he would make himself gag. Jaden was still in a pull-up, he was walking but was wobbly on his feet, and he still had very poor fine motor skills. His communications skills were lacking. Jaden could say about seven words and sign about thirty-five, and because his communication skills were lacking, he was also lacking academically.

We didn't have all of the answers. We knew Jaden had low muscle tone and therefore weak fine and gross motor skills, but we didn't know why. We knew he was virtually deaf, but we didn't know why. We knew he still had what I call "Jaden quirks," but we were still on a mission to find answers. Though in my head I knew it wasn't so, at times I wondered. *Was it indeed the falling off my bed all of those years ago that caused all of this.* We were on a mission to find out answers, but in the meantime Jaden's new team would need to work with what they had. They had issues to address, even if they didn't have the answers to all the why's.

In the past, I had been very used to being able to watch Jaden's EI therapies, so I knew what to do with him at home. The only therapy I had not really been able to watch was physical therapy; we were basically banned from his PT sessions, because if Jaden saw us he would cry and quit working for Mike. Once Mike got Jaden into "the zone," Jaden worked hard. Jaden was determined and focused, but as soon as he saw Mom or Dad—forget about it. I've ruined more than a session or two by getting caught by Jaden spying on him. Even if I missed all of his therapies in any given week, I was in touch with and spoke with all of his therapists several times a week, and Glenn was always there, so he could tell me what they did, too, and what I needed to be working on.

School, now that would be different. Jaden didn't talk, and we wouldn't be there, and so how the heck would we know how this boy was doing in school? That is where his teacher was a godsend. There was the communication book; a notebook that goes back and forth from home to school telling about the child's day at school. I relied on that to keep me up to date, and of course I usually get more info about the goings-on at school from the communication book than I do from Jaden himself.

Chapter 14

Jaden went to school for a week, started to get the swing of things, then got pneumonia and was out for a week. He did, however, seem to enjoy school, and the notes home were for the most part all positive, though he surely had things to work on. Reading through his communication book for those early days in school, some things in particular make me laugh.

1/15/10: Jaden ate 3 M&M's today. Asked for more ☺ He does close his eyes when it goes in his mouth. Maybe not used to them?

Thanks to Cathy Lee, my child has a sweet tooth that began with his teacher and M&M's.

01/19/10: LOTS of closing his eyes w/Gail. Got him to eat two cheerios during oral motor though. So baby steps ☺ After Gail left he was fine. No more closing his eyes."

Yep, his new team was getting familiar with my odd, quirky child.

The positive notes kept on coming, including things like

Jaden was all smiles today! Doing well identifying some of the kids' names, especially the girls☺

and

ate 8 M&M's today with the biggest smile☺. I make him sign and vocalize for them. He prefers to sign and not vocalize. I make him do both. Doesn't like it, but can do it and will for an M&M.

We fell in love with Jaden's teacher, his classmates, and all of those who worked with Jaden. A mom of a deaf kid's dream come true, I now had an audiologist to go to every time I was curious about this or that, and I could ask any question that popped into my head. I no longer had to wait until Jaden's next hearing evaluation to ask my questions, and thanks to all of Cathy's and Gail's efforts Jaden's communication skills were improving by leaps and bounds. Sure, lots of the notes that came home stating that he had cried and/or shut his eyes during speech therapy, but I didn't care because whatever Gail was doing was working.

Chapter 15

We were still on the hunt for answers as to why Jaden was the way he was, and so we had been referred to an ear, nose, and throat (ENT) specialist. In February 2010, Jaden would have a CAT scan done, and another ABR test would be performed, but this time under sedation. Because we were no longer confident in our local hospital shortly after Jaden's diagnosis, we had switched audiologists. For quite some time by this point, we had been seeing the audiology group who worked with the ENT Jaden was referred to. Their office was in Syracuse, about an hour away from our home. The car rides were long, but for better care it was well worth the trip.

The CAT scan was being performed because it could possibly provide answers as to why Jaden is deaf. The ABR was being done because, since Jaden was already going to be put under sedation for the CAT scan, his audiologist thought it might be a good idea to repeat the test. Because the ABR would be done this time under sedation, there would be no struggling to keep Jaden still and quiet, and perhaps the results would be more informative this time around.

Because Jaden was still getting over having had pneumonia and needed to be healthy for the tests, they had to be canceled and rescheduled more than once. Finally, on February 18, at just a few days shy of Jaden's third birthday, we kissed our baby on the head and let the doctor wheel him away to go under anesthesia and begin the tests.

The ABR tests came back with the same results as the original: Jaden had a severe to profound hearing loss in the right ear and a moderate loss in the left ear. The findings of the CT: "Bilateral Mondini's malformation with ectasia of the vestibule and lateral semicircular canal bilaterally which are likely fused." To explain, inside the ear is a snail-like bony structure called the cochlea. In Mondini's malformation, part of the cochlea is missing or incomplete.

We now knew why Jaden was deaf. I could no longer think in the back of my head that perhaps it was due to his falling off the bed when he was less than a year old. Without a doubt, Mondini's malformation was why Jaden couldn't hear.

This new information explained Jaden's hearing loss and also some of his balance issues, as balance is commonly affected by Mondini's malformation. I remember a note coming home one day saying Jaden had toppled over while doing the song "Head, Shoulders, Knees, and Toes" and that he didn't want to continue after that; he didn't have good enough balance to bend over to touch his toes. This newfound information still didn't explain Jaden's low muscle tone and several other Jaden quirks, however, we hadn't really expected to get answers to all of our questions from the CT and ABR tests.

The new knowledge was good and useful to have in our back pocket and to be aware of, but it didn't really change a thing. If anything, this new information let us know we were already doing the things we needed to do and that we should keep on doing them. Jaden had been getting speech and physical therapies for years now, along with his other therapies, so nothing new was needed in the treatment department. Nonetheless I was happy to know what had caused Jaden's deafness. *Now,* I thought, *if we could only unlock our child's other mysteries.*

Chapter 16

Tons of positive things were happening, but I wouldn't be telling the full story if I failed to say that during those early months of 2010 Glenn and I doubted our decision to send Jaden to school more than a time or two. Jaden was a boy who in the past was tuckered out by EI therapy throughout the day but got all energized again via a one- to two-hour hour nap at home every day. Now Jaden's days were much, much longer. The bus came to get him a little before seven in the morning and he didn't get home until about four in the afternoon; at school there would be no one- to two-hour nap every day, just a rest period in the afternoon, when some kids would nap and others would lie there quietly. Given Jaden's long, action-packed days, by Wednesday and Thursday evening we had a cranky, overtired, miserable monster on our hands.

It didn't help that though things were improved we were still struggling in the communication department. Jaden would want something, and we oftentimes couldn't figure out what it was, and then there would be a meltdown and temper tantrum to follow. Then there were the days where Jaden would come home and fall asleep, we'd fight with him to wake him for dinner and a bath if needed, and then he'd go right back to sleep. Also Jaden wasn't used to being around so many other kids and their germs, so it seemed that every time another child got sick he did, too. Jaden ended up missing school due to being ill quite a bit his first school year. Yes, I wondered a time or two if we should have waited until September to start school, those first few months were an adjustment for everyone, Mom, Dad, Jaden, and those who worked with him at school. But the many, many pros far outweighed the few cons. Jaden was slowly turning into a new little boy.

Jaden's school didn't have a physical therapist his first year there, but God bless his occupational therapist. Her name was Andrea Rounds, and she was a saint! Andrea addressed Jaden's many fine motor needs. He was working on fine motor skills such as properly holding a pencil, completing puzzles, and stringing beads, but when and where possible she helped Jaden work on gross motor issues, too. Not only was Andrea helping my boy work on fine and gross motor skills but she also began the slow process of helping Jaden expand his ever so limited food choices.

Jaden had had a few feeding evaluations, and aside from his having low muscle tone in his jaw/maxofacial area, there were no medical reasons for his limited food choices. This was just one of Jaden's many "Jaden quirks." If he liked something, he would eat it. If he didn't, he would refuse it and/or make himself gag. I remember one time when pizza was offered at a family birthday party. Jaden cried at the sight of it. No one had said he had to have any, no one had even offered him any. He just saw the pizza, knew he didn't like or want it, and burst into tears at the simple sight of it.

Working on feeding issues was a joint effort between Glenn and me; Andrea; and Jaden's eventual K/1 teacher, Theresa Matt, but the true initiator of helping Jaden in this area was Andrea. First, Andrea would begin to coax Jaden to smell an item, eventually he would touch the item with his tongue, and at long last he would take at least one small bite of the item being offered. It took a few years, but eventually Jaden would expand his food choices.

In his first experience with school, Jaden had adjusted quite nicely. Looking back at his communication books and report cards between January and June 2010, I remember that he had quite a few successes, such as learning to spell his name as well as classmates' names, learning to vocalize and use sign, and learning to label and identify objects in his environment. He was still often cranky and tired by midweek, but all things considered he was doing great. He seemed really to enjoy and thrive in school, and so we opted to send him to summer school. He would continue learning throughout the summer and would also continue getting speech and occupational therapy as well.

A few things made me slightly nervous about sending Jaden to summer school. We didn't want Jaden to miss out on the therapies that he needed, the learning opportunities that would be provided, or the chance to play and have fun with his new friends, but then again Jaden didn't and doesn't always adapt very well to change. For half of summer school, he would have Cathy Lee, and for the other half of summer school the teacher Theresa Matt, would be new to him. How would our boy do with this new teacher? I was also worried about his speech therapy. The last time a note was sent home saying Jaden didn't corporate with Gail was on April 27:

> Jaden was stubborn w/Gail. She moved him to a straight face from a happy face, so he lost his prize. Sad face from him, but maybe he will make the connection.

The note the very next day said,

> He made the connection and did *real* well in speech today. Hopefully that is all it will take.

From that moment on, there has not been a note saying he cried with Gail, he hid from Gail, he refused to go with Gail, he closed his eyes and wouldn't look at Gail or anything of the sorts. Summer school would be with a new speech therapist. Was he in for a miserable summer with both a new speech therapist and a new classroom teacher for half of the summer?

Our concerns were quickly relieved as we were told

> . . . Jaden did well in speech. No crying at all! He is maturing☺

And in August, when Theresa took over summer school. Jaden did well for her, too:

> . . . Jaden had a lot of fun today learning about flowers and vegetable gardens . . .

Summer school was a good experience for him. Arts and crafts, music, swimming, picnics, and more all mixed in with learning, and to boot he still got his speech and occupational therapy.

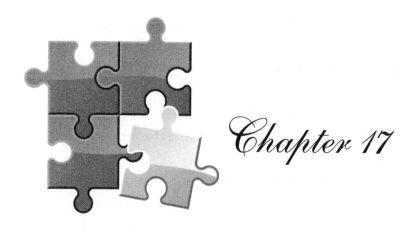

Chapter 17

It was late summer and things were pretty hectic in the Roback house. There was the business of getting ready for school, which would soon be starting again, and Glenn and I were still working on expanding our family. We'd been trying for months to conceive with no success. I had been to my ob-gyn's office and we had discussed my getting pregnant. I was advised that because of how Jaden's delivery went and because of several clots found in my placenta after his birth that I would be considered high risk, but my doctor was okay with our moving forward with infertility treatments.

Glenn and I both would undergo infertility testing, which included labs for him and some labs and other not so fun tests for me. After all testing was complete, I was placed on a fertility medication and Glenn and I decided to proceed with artificial insemination. There were two disastrous attempts at artificial insemination, the details of which I'll save for another book, but to make a semi-short story even shorter I will say this: I never ended up making it to either scheduled appointment, the second of which I neither showed up for nor called to cancel. I haven't been back to or in contact with that medical office since then; I mean, who wants to treat a patient who no-call, no-shows? I wouldn't. It caused much tension between Glenn and me, and ultimately I decided I couldn't do it. I couldn't go through another debacle like the first two attempts, so that would be the end of any artificial insemination attempts. We would continue to try, but on our own.

Jaden was continuing to do great! I suspect that most parents, when their child is disrespectful and/or talks back to them, discipline their child in some way. In August of 2010, just before the new school year began, Jaden was disrespectful to me, but unlike most parents in such a situation, I had to leave the room to jump for joy and smile without his seeing me.

Jaden was playing with a toy and had become upset for one reason or another and he threw the toy. I gave him a time-out, and as he was sitting in time-out I explained to him why we don't throw toys. "Jaden, you could have broken the toy or you could have hit and hurt someone—" Jaden looked at me and attempted to say, "Chair time. Not ears time," as he took his hearing aids off and handed them to me. His words were only partially intelligible, but his signs and actions were very well understood. He wanted me to know it was time for him to sit in time-out but not to listen to Mom running her mouth.

It was the first time our child used four words at once to communicate at home. My first and immediate thought was *Hip hip hooray*. This was a breakthrough, and I wanted to jump up and down and do a happy dance. My second thought was *Don't let Jaden see me smile . . . Don't let Jaden see me smile.* And then I realized, *I can't have this kid taking his hearing aids off every time he doesn't want to listen. What the heck am I going to do now?*

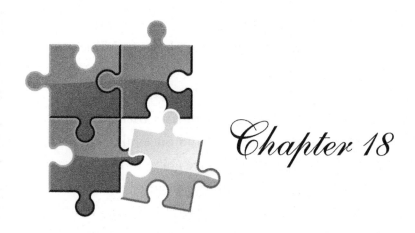

Chapter 18

September came and the new school year began. Jaden had been going for hearing testing every three to six months, and based on his most recent hearing testing it was determined that his hearing aid on the right side was no longer helping him at all. With his right hearing aid turned up to its highest level, the boy was hearing zilch, zero, nada, but everyone else was hearing lots of annoying feedback due to how high the hearing aid was turned up. Because of this, in September of 2010 Jaden would begin to wear only one hearing aid, on his left side. The hearing in Jaden's left ear had been pretty stable since his original diagnosis, with only slight decreases in his hearing ability here and there, and his hearing aid helps him out greatly on that side.

To this day, hearing evaluations are one thing I've never quite gotten used to. Should Glenn and I continue to hope Jaden's hearing stays status quo, knowing that he's done really well having the benefit of hearing only on his left side? Or should we hope for his hearing to decrease a little bit more, just enough so that he qualifies for a cochlear implant? Then he would have an implant on his right side and a hearing aid on his left side and would therefore have the benefit of bilateral hearing. Which do you wish for?

It's a double-edged sword. Part of me feels that for Jaden to have bilateral hearing would be huge gain. As a friend of mine, Kirstin Hubley who also has a deaf son and once said, "You try walking around with one eye closed. You're going to miss out on a lot. It's the same with hearing," meaning it would be immensely helpful for a child like Jaden to have bilateral hearing. Another part of me feels like he's done really well without an implant, and all surgeries have risks and not all surgeries are successes, so which do you wish for?

Jaden was off to a good start of this new school year. Notes came home saying things like

Talking lots here. I am understanding him more and more.

Among his other quirks, however, he was still not potty trained. Many of the notes that went back and forth between home and school that fall were about getting Jaden potty trained. It wasn't until his teacher shared a book with me that she had used with her own daughter that we had a breakthrough. The book was *3 Day Potty Training*, by Lora Jensen, and it worked, or at least for Jaden it did. It took longer than three days for him to get it, but the method in that book helped greatly.

10/13/10: Cathy was out sick today. I'm so proud of Jaden! Around 1:40 PM he signed "potty." I placed him on the toilet—YEAH—he went in the toilet.

Six days later I wrote this note to the teachers at school:

. . . Here it goes. Going to send him with his undies on. Hopefully he will do ok . . .

There were some accidents and kinks to work out, but by December/January he finally had it down pat; there were no accidents; after that and he was comfortable enough to use the facilities at school any time he needed them.

Jaden was also continuing to mature and grow in other areas. He was still eating primarily stage 3 baby food, but he had recently begun accepting at least a few bites of chicken here and there. He was a work in progress. His speech and sign were continuing to improve, he was making slight gains in his use of fine motor skills, and in November he would finally start physical therapy again. He still, however, had his Jaden quirks.

For example, he didn't like to pose. I was pretty excited for Jaden's first school pictures. Because he had started school in January 2010, and so missed out on school pictures taken the previous fall, these would be his first ever school pictures. We sent him to school dressed up and looking handsome, and then he came home with a note that said,

We tried to get Jaden's picture. We went over two different times. Had him watch the other kids, see their pictures, etc. He wouldn't do it. Crying and carrying on, head down. Even tried having him sit on one of our laps. I am sorry . . .

The next year he did at least get his school picture taken, but they were horrid! Tears in his eyes and a huge pout face, and that was after having been bribed with M&M's. My quirky stubborn child, I would have to wait until kindergarten to get a decent school picture of Jaden.

Chapter 19

October and November 2010 would be big months for Jaden. He had his first dental checkup, which failed miserably, as he cried and wouldn't open his mouth. He had another hearing evaluation. He had an appointment to get a new ear mold for his hearing aid. He was beginning physical therapy again. And at long last he would see a geneticist, which was an appointment we had scheduled back in March at Jaden's three-year well-child check-up. Many of the mysteries of Jaden had yet to be unlocked and Jaden's pediatrician thought that seeing a geneticist could possibly provide us with more pieces of the puzzle.

On October 28 we headed to Syracuse for the genetics appointment. Would we finally unlock the remaining mysteries of Jaden? Would the cause of Jaden's other issues such as his low muscle tone, feeding issues, and social oddities finally be revealed? It was a very interesting appointment. To witness every inch of my child being observed, graded, and documented was very unique experience. Everything was noted, the flatness on the back of his head, the shape and slanting of his eyes, the structure and narrowness of his nose, that he has a webbed toe on each foot, his birthmarks, muscle tone, social interaction or in this case lack thereof. All were noted in addition to many, many other things.

I went into the appointment thinking I had a normal-looking, cute little kid. I left the appointment with knowledge that Jaden displays physical characteristics that would be helpful in narrowing down the scope of testing needed. His physical differences are subtle and not as obvious as those commonly seen in those with other genetic conditions such as Down syndrome, for example. But nonetheless the doctors confirmed Jaden had some of the physical features that are commonly seen in other genetic diseases. The plan was that after the appointment that day, Jaden would have blood drawn for genetic testing. We would follow back up with the geneticist in one year, unless the blood work identified issues that needed to be addressed.

We went upstairs to the lab at the hospital to have Jaden's blood drawn. This was a terrible experience for Glenn, myself, and most of all for Jaden. When he was younger, I would always make Glenn do the dirty job of holding Jaden for shots, blood work, and anything else painful. I didn't want to hold my baby while someone was hurting him. So this time while Glenn was holding Jaden, the lab person poked his arm and missed the vein. Jaden began to cry of course. This happened two more times, and at this point our baby was in pain, screaming and crying, and Glenn got quite upset and let the lab person know she needed to get someone else to draw Jaden's blood, someone who knew how to draw blood from small children. The woman said she was the only one in the lab at the time, but if we wanted, we could go to another lab a few blocks away.

After leaving the hospital and making a few wrong turns along the way, we finally made it to the new lab. Thank God we didn't have too long of a wait there, and technician there was able to get Jaden's blood on first attempt. They also loaded him up with stickers in an attempt to make him feel better afterward. The blood work needed to be sent to a specialized lab that did the genetic testing Jaden needed, so we would have to wait about a week before getting any results. We headed back home, and now the waiting game would begin.

Chapter 20

On November 8 Glenn got the call while I was at work. Shortly thereafter, I received an e-mail from him letting me know the geneticist's office had called him, he'd been told Jaden had a microdeletion in chromosome number 22, and that Jaden would need to come in for a follow-up appointment, which was scheduled for November 17. Between the date of the call informing us of the genetic information and the date of Jaden's appointment, we were like little FBI agents scouring the Internet for any research and information that we could find.

One site would refer to this deletion as DeGeorge syndrome, another as Velocardiofacial syndrome (VCFS), and other sites listed yet different names. What did Jaden have? One of these syndromes? All of them? Some of the things we read were scary and confusing and included long lists of medical symptoms and problems. I couldn't help but think, *What did I get us into? Did I push too hard and too much for answers?* It didn't matter, as there was no turning back now.

We walked into the clinic on that November day with a list of questions in hand. From the geneticist, we found out that DeGeorge syndrome and VCFS are essentially one and the same. Different doctors had first described and treated patients for different symptoms, which led to more than one name being given for the same syndrome. It was later that discovered that all of these patients had a deletion in chromosome 22. More recently, there has been a name change, and today the syndrome is more commonly referred to as 22q11.2 syndrome, or simply 22q for short. We were told Jaden has a smaller deletion than what most with 22q have, and that only two or three years earlier the technology to diagnose a deletion such as his had not even existed. Jaden was diagnosed thanks to the advent of something called chromosomal microarray technology.

We were told that because of this, "few patients have been identified with the same deletion as Jaden. It is possible that Jaden's only clinical concerns resulting from this deletion may be his hearing loss and mild developmental delays. However, because we do not know what the implications are, we would like his family to be aware of the concerns that can occur in patients with the traditional 22q11 deletion."

We were able to meet with Dr. Robert Shprintzen, a renowned clinician and researcher in the 22q world, credited as being one of the first to describe and treat patients with 22q. He explained to us that because so little is known about the kind of deletion Jaden has, the answers to a lot of our questions are truly unknown. Some patients develop mental illnesses such as schizophrenia; others have medical issues such as seizures, heart problems, kidney problems, immune deficiency weaknesses, thyroid problems, feeding problems, and a whole host of other problems they wanted us to be aware of because they didn't know if Jaden had or would develop these symptoms. We were also told that hearing loss is at times seen in those with 22q, as are feeding issues and low muscle tone.

Jaden would be referred for several tests. He would now need an echocardiogram to check on his heart, a renal ultrasound to check on his kidneys, another feeding evaluation to address his eating habits, a thyroid screening to check the function of his thyroid, and a complete blood count with platelets in addition to follow-up care with the International Velocardiofacial Syndrome Center at SUNY Upstate Medical University in Syracuse.

Glenn and I were informed that it is possible Jaden inherited the deleted chromosome from one of his parents, and that unless we were to both undergo genetic testing no one would be able to tell which one of us had passed on the deleted chromosome. The genetic testing is quite costly and is not covered by insurance, so we opted not to do it. Without the genetic testing, we were told that determining whether a future child would have 22q syndrome was like flipping a coin: a future child would have a fifty-fifty chance of having 22q, and if the child did have 22q there is no way of knowing how severe his or her symptoms would be. The child could have symptoms such as Jaden's or any of the much more severe and oftentimes life-threatening symptoms often associated with 22q, such as heart complications and cleft pallet, among other things. We were also told that Jaden will have a 50 percent chance of passing 22q on to any future children he may have.

It was all I could do to hold it together in the doctor's office. I felt my voice cracking and remember thinking to myself, *Don't cry . . .don't cry . . .* I did indeed manage to keep it together. But I was saddened, for I knew in that moment the course of our future would forever be changed. I was saddened because I knew then that there would be no more babies for Glenn and me. I was worried for Jaden. What would his future entail? I wished then that I had not been so pushy to get to the bottom of Jaden's issues.

We left the appointment and headed back toward home. It was a long and quiet ride home. Silent tears fell from my cheeks as I would occasionally peek at Jaden in the rearview mirror. About halfway home I blurted out, "If you want to stop trying for another baby. I am okay with that." Glenn said nothing.

I sent Cathy Lee a long-winded e-mail giving her the scoop on Jaden and wrote a note in the communication book saying,

> We got lots of info, lots of future appointments to go to, lots of answers and lots of things to be on the lookout for in the future. Some things worry me, but overall it was a good appointment . . .

That "we got lots of info" part was true, but in my head I was thinking that the appointment had gone horribly. I called my mom that night in tears and said, "I can't do it anymore. I can't do it; I want good news for once and a normal child." My mom just assured me that God wouldn't have given me Jaden if I couldn't do it. It's interesting the things that bother or don't bother a person. I can truly say that when we found out about Jaden's being deaf I was not bothered by it. I was upset with myself for not knowing beforetime and for the time he had missed out on hearing but not with the deafness itself. I jumped right in on getting hearing aids and getting Joan on our team. I should have been the same way with this, but I wasn't. On the outside, I was busy making appointments and doing what needed to be done, but on the inside I was falling apart at the seams. I finally had the answers I had long been searching for, and yet I wasn't content or happy with our newfound knowledge; I was instead devastated. I was unable to see at the time that we had indeed been given good news.

Chapter 21

As I oftentimes tend to communicate better in print than in person, I e-mailed Glenn about a week after the appointment in Syracuse, letting him know that I was serious about what I had blurted out in the car on the way home, that if he no longer wanted to continue trying for another child, I understood. He waited awhile before replying to me, probably to make sure I wasn't going to change my mind. A few weeks later, Glenn sent me an e-mail letting me know the story that a neighbor of his dad's had told him a few years prior. His dad's neighbor was an elderly woman who had two grown children, one special needs child followed by another child who was not special needs. The neighbor told Glenn that though she of course loved both of her children with all of her heart, part of her had always wished she had not had a second child. Though the second child was born without special needs, the woman felt that the special needs child took too much time away from the second child, and therefore the second child was shortchanged on time and attention.

Glenn apparently felt the same way. Actually he had felt this way for a few years now; he had only been going along with trying to have another child because that is what I wanted. Part of me was angry, hurt, and furious with this information. Part of me felt, *You're just telling me this now! Why didn't you share this with me years ago when I first wanted to try for another child? No wonder why we haven't gotten pregnant and the two appointments for artificial insemination were huge failures that I didn't even make it to.* I also didn't agree with his feelings. I was no longer ready for another child, but it had nothing to do with Jaden being "special needs." As I've said, I've never actually considered him special needs. My reasons for no longer wanting another child were because I was afraid of having another child with 22q, one who could potentially have any one of the more severe and potentially life-threating health issues associated with the syndrome that Jaden is so fortunate not to have.

Yes, I felt angry and hurt, but I have also always been huge on open and honest communication, so I also felt, *Wow! I don't agree with your reasons for not wanting another child, but you are being so open and honest with me, which is what I've always wanted. I appreciate that! You can't help the way you feel, and I am thankful that you are sharing this with me even if I would have rather known your feelings sooner.* So we never had an argument over this new information, and I never said I was angry or hurt over this information being shared with me so belatedly. Instead I just thanked Glenn for being open and honest with me, and for a very long time aside from the odd joke now and then, that was the end of any baby-making talk.

December 2010 and January 2011 were busy months for us. Jaden had his EKG and renal ultrasound, both of which thankfully came back normal. There would also be feeding evaluations and lab appointments, too, add into the mix his regularly scheduled hearing evaluation, and an appointment to pick up his new ear mold plus all of the normal holiday hustle and bustle in preparation for the upcoming holidays. It was a busy few months. After all of the craziness was done, after all appointments were over and results were back (all normal), I was also finally able to look at Jaden's diagnosis as a good thing. We now had the answers I had long been searching for.

The puzzle that is Jaden was now complete. I now knew why Jaden didn't truly begin to walk until after he was two. His feeding quirks finally made sense. Why he struggles with fine and gross motor control now was clear. All of these things are because of 22q. We know Jaden will always have low muscle tone, and so physical and occupational therapy will be in his long-term future. We had long known that Jaden was deaf, so hearing aids and, should his hearing ever decrease to the degree that he qualifies for the procedure, cochlear implants will be needed. We know to continue with speech therapy and to monitor his hearing. We know to take baby steps with feeding and that he will likely always be a picky eater. Though not related to 22q, for years we had also known about the arachnoid cyst and what the potential complications because of it are. By golly, if these are the only issues Jaden has, then we can deal with that. Heck, we'd already been dealing with it for years. We know the things to be on the lookout for in the future. Sure, he could have a mental illness;

sure, future health issues may arise, but then again they may not and we now had the knowledge of what to be aware of.

It may have taken me a few months to feel positive about things, but Jaden's diagnosis was a good thing because it brought us knowledge and information. The key pieces of who Jaden is were now known to us. Aside from experiencing a hectic few months with lots of appointments to go to, there weren't really any changes in how we needed to care for Jaden. As with his earlier diagnosis of Mondini's malformation, the new diagnosis confirmed for us that we were already doing everything we needed to do for this boy.

Each of Jaden's issues needed to be addressed separately from the others, as its own separate issue, and we were already doing that. Jaden was already getting speech therapy and being seen by an audiologist to address hearing and speech issues, he was already being seen by an occupational therapist to address fine motor needs, he had recently begun physical therapy services again to address gross motor needs, and of course he was seen by his pediatrician for colds and minor illnesses. We were on the right track.

Chapter 22

In January 2011, Jaden, who was approaching four years of age, had been in school for a year now and was doing well. Academically, he was on track; he was smart and knew the things a child his age should know. With the help of Andrea, his occupational therapist, he was continuing to make small gains in fine motor skills. He had just recently begun physical therapy again and that was a bit more of a challenge. A note came home saying,

> In P.T. the therapist had him working on a tricycle. Jaden got *so upset* he was in fetal position crying and biting his hands. He finally calmed down and she was able to work with him. They went around the gym a few times . . . I think he was afraid he would fall . . .

A few other notes home were similar in nature.

Andrea attended P.T. with Jaden so he would be more comfortable and work for the therapist . . .

Yes, he would need to get used to his new therapist and learn to trust her.

As he had been in the fall, Jaden was still eating primarily stage three baby food, but his food choices were continuing to expand. As for his speech, this, too, was improving. Sure, there were still communication barriers and issues to overcome, including temper tantrums when communication broke down as they did on January 15 when he was promised a trip to Toys 'R' Us to use a gift card he had received—only for me to realize upon arrival at the store that I'd left the card at home and we would need to go home to get it. Jaden did not understand that we would be going back to the store after going home to get the card, and that is when he melted down. In the backseat of the car, he had a screaming fit, and during this tantrum he took his hearing aid apart and threw his ear mold Lord only knows where, as it was never found and we had to make a doctor's appointment to have a new one made.

January 2011 also happens to be the month I was given what I consider to be the best gift I have received aside from the gift that is Jaden. Jaden said *Mama*.

He had been working with Gail since January 2010, and in January 2011, at three years and eleven months, thanks to his wonderful speech therapist, I finally got to hear him address me as his mom. One word that was so small, and yet how I had longed to hear it. Gail earned rock-star status in my book that day.

Sure, I knew that Jaden knew who I was and that he loved me. He had long been signing the word *mama*, and he had been able to voice "I love you" for quite some time, but at this point Jaden still didn't have many words in his vocabulary. In ways that could be easily understood by those familiar with Jaden and his speech patterns, he could say the names of several animals, the names of several classmates, *Dad*, the names of his brother and sister, those of some of his aunts and uncles, and a bunch of other words, too, so darn it all, I deeply wanted to hear Jaden pronounce the *mmm* sounds as in *Mama*.

I had wanted to hear it and at three years and eleven months, and at every interval since. Following much effort, time, and dedication put into teaching Jaden by his speech therapist, it happened. After he began saying the word, I took a short video in which I asked Jaden, "Jaden, who am I?" just so that I could hear him say, "Mom, Mama, Mama," and—I kid you not—I went around the house like that for weeks, randomly asking him, "Who am I?" just so I could hear him say "Mama." Yes, that is the best gift I have ever been given aside from Jaden, and I credit Gail for it.

A more recent photo of Jaden and Gail

Chapter 23

Jaden, Cathy and Nancy during a birthday party for Jaden at school

In February 2011 Jaden would be turning four. He was to celebrate his birthday at school with cupcakes, ice cream cups, and goodie bags for the kids. Glenn and I were also invited to come and celebrate with his class. I was excited to get to partake in his school birthday party; however, because that day Jaden became ill while at school, threw up, and came home sick, his party was postponed until after midwinter recess. Glenn and I would still come to school with the above-mentioned treats and help Jaden celebrate his birthday with his classmates.

I have mentioned previously that Jaden could be at times socially awkward. He had a habit of hiding, looking down, making minimal eye contact when he didn't feel comfortable with a person, place, or situation. That wasn't just with strangers; the social awkwardness extended to family, too, as in right on down to Mom and Dad. Jaden's school party ended up being on March 3, and we arrived at school that afternoon with treats in hand only to have Jaden hide under a table and cry huge tears at the sight of us. I'm not sure if he thought we were at school to bring him home, or if he just thought Mom and Dad didn't belong at school, but whatever he was thinking he surely didn't want us there. As we wanted him to enjoy his party, come out of hiding, and play with his friends, Glenn and I opted to leave the party and to go and watch the action from the observation room. We were still able to see all of the action, just without Jaden knowing we were there. Toward the end of the party, we reentered the classroom and were able to watch from a distance.

In the spring it seemed four-year-old Jaden's speech was improving by leaps and bounds. I began keeping track of and oftentimes sharing what I call "Jaden funnies." I kept track of things with diary entries such as

04/03/2011: At McDonald's Playland Jaden felt the need to identify everyone by "man," "lady," "boy," or "girl." Jaden gets to one man and says and signs very loud and clear "OLD MAN." How embarrassing."

and

04/04/11: On a nature walk today Jaden began yelling "Birds, where are you?" Scared them all away, I don't think being a great nature walk boy is in his future.

I found many of the things Jaden said to be really funny, and I didn't take any of it for granted. He was now doing something that for a very long time we didn't know if he would ever do. Jaden was using speech in his communication more and more and ever more intelligibly. There was no comparing the Jaden who started pre-K in January 2010 to the new little boy we had in 2011. Sure Jaden had a long way to go, but he was already a brand-new little boy.

In spring of 2011, I developed a new hobby in part thanks to Cathy Lee. Jaden's class was learning about tadpoles and was raising them. I had never really been a baker and certainly never tried decorating anything fancy or cute. I saw frog cupcakes and decided I would for the first time attempt fancy cupcakes to celebrate the tadpoles. The frog cupcakes Jaden and I made were a big hit, which led to my newfound hobby of decorating cakes and cupcakes. I began to send in my attempts at fancy, cute decorated cupcakes or cakes about once a week. I'm well aware it wasn't the healthiest of choices to send in, but I was on a roll with this newfound hobby. Eventually, I would send in cakes only rarely and would instead try to opt for healthier options!

The school year would soon be coming to an end, and Jaden had progressed so much. He loved school and those working with him, there were no longer notes saying he was looking down and making minimal eye contact instead notes said things such as

Lots of hugs from Jaden lately . . .

and

I was surprised that Jaden touched a turtle today when the zoo mobile came

and

Had a visit from Marquis' dog and Jaden petted it this time! *WOW.*

His report card had notes and comments such as Jaden has shown so much growth in so many areas this year. He has become more assertive and has tried and attempted things this year that he would have never tried before . . .

Another school year had come to a close, and what a great year it had been for Jaden.

Chapter 24

Summer came and went, in between family camping trips and other summertime activities. Jaden also attended summer school, just as he had done the year prior. Before we would know it, fall would be here and it would be time for school to resume. Jaden was only four in September of 2011, so he would again be in Cathy Lee's Little Listeners pre-K class. He was thriving, thanks to Cathy Lee. He had developed a love of school and learning that has lasted ever since. I would often hear comments such as the ones he made to me on September 27: "Mama, I happy. I had school today, sleep now, wake up and more school. I like school."

I've never thought that Jaden no longer benefiting from use of a hearing aid on his right side as a good thing, but Jaden still having it as a spare aid did come in handy once upon a time.

10/05/11: What a day! On our walk back from lunch somewhere, somehow, Jaden's hearing aid came apart from his tube and ear mold. He told Nancy, but when we retraced our steps we could not find it. I told Kim and we resumed the search. Jaden was so upset. I gave him a hug and he did calm down and returned to class okay. I know Kim called you. We feel so bad! Hopefully it will turn up.

Yep, losing a hearing aid stank. You may not know, but for such a tiny item they are quite costly, and in this one instance Jaden no longer using a hearing aid on his right side came in handy for him. We had his old right hearing aid, and we were thankfully able to use that spare hearing aid, so aside from that one day in class that Jaden's was lost, he didn't have to go without a hearing aid.

About a month later, on November 2, the missing hearing aid was found by one of Jaden's classmates while playing on the playground. Not only was it found, but it had been in a semi-sheltered area so despite having been exposed to quite rainy wet weather, the hearing aid still worked! Talk about having luck on your side!

We started bringing Jaden to swimming at school on Monday evenings that fall. We were hoping that it would be good for a few things. First, we hoped that Jaden would benefit from exposure to being with other kids as much as possible. Second, swimming was good for his muscles. And third, he was still not happy when Mom and Dad came to school, so we hoped that with Mom taking him to school and being there with him once a week, he would get the message that it's okay to see Mom and Dad at school and that it's also okay to see friends outside of school. Our ulterior motives kind of worked. Jaden now did okay when seeing Glenn or I at school. He was always slightly shy and reserved, but there was no crying and/or hiding. However, he was still thrown off if we happened to bump into a classmate or staff member outside of school. He would look down and not speak to them, so though it turned out to be a great thing for Jaden, my bringing him to school every Monday evening for swimming didn't achieve all of our goals.

Chapter 25

Fall had gone and winter had come, and nothing significant was going on with Jaden. He continued to get speech, physical, and occupational therapies, he had routine doctor's appointments, there were hearing evaluations and appointments with his pediatrician when he got sick, and he was on and off a nebulizer (a mister used for delivery of medication) as needed, but that was nothing out the ordinary for Jaden. He was doing well in school again this year. He had developed a newfound love of asking questions. Gail had taught Jaden how to ask them, and I am sure she regretted it a time a two. I know I did! Comments on his report card read as follows:

> Jaden wins the prize for most questions asked in one day! In one week! . . .

For every answer you would give Jaden, he would have another question to ask. His love of questions lasted throughout the school year with comments on later report cards reading,

The latest language I get in Group Speech is "I have a question for you." Who knew a 5-year-old would give a warning like that?! . . .

Soon it would be February and Jaden would be five. Jaden had come such a long long way since starting NYSSD two years ago. Part of this I am certain is due to the normal growing and maturing all children go through over time but a much larger part of Jaden's many successes was due to the team behind him. Jaden continued to make small gains with his gross and fine motor skills. He continued to improve by leaps and bounds academically and with his speech, too. All of this progress is due to the time, effort, and dedication put into my boy by his team. There however were certain things that would still send Jaden over the edge, such as textures he didn't like. His speech, though much improved, was limited. He could still be socially awkward, and at almost five years old he was still eating baby food.

I could no longer take it. It was awkward being out to eat with family and getting stares when Jaden would be eating baby food—looks that in my mind said, "What in the heck!?" So I did it, I lied to my kid. It was about a week after his fifth birthday, and I told him, "Grandma knows a baby named Thomas. Thomas's mommy and daddy don't have any food for him, and you are a big boy now, so we are going to pack up all of your baby food and give it to Grandma for baby Thomas." Is lying to your kid the best approach? Nope, but I didn't want the meltdown that would surely ensue if I just got rid of his food for no reason. Jaden was a sweet boy, and if he thought he was helping someone, he might just go along with it. He was hesitant, but—knock on wood—he went with it. I had Jaden help me pack up his food, and we said good-bye to it.

Visions of being turned in for child neglect or abuse were now running through my head. Jaden was already underweight. *Would he starve now? Would he loose even more weight? Were we in for more fits of gagging and throwing up when he didn't want to eat something offered to him? Was this the right choice? He's gotta eat if he gets hungry enough, right?* His diet would now be even more limited. At least in the baby food variety he would eat things like spaghetti and sauce, meatballs, chicken and vegetables, and more. In big-kid foods, he was eating very, very limitedly, primarily peanut butter on bread or peanut butter on crackers, no cheese, no sauce, no pasta, and the list of no to this and that goes on and on. At first I was worried that he was five and still eating baby food, now I was constantly worried about whether he was getting enough nutrition. It was almost as if we were back to the newborn days of keeping track of how many ounces of formula he got and when he got it. I was now journaling what he ate, when, and how much. What in the world would I feed this kid now? It didn't matter, I had to come up with something to feed this boy.

It was indeed a struggle at first, and to the present Jaden remains what I consider to be a picky eater. It's only been more recently that he's expanded his food choices and become more willing to at least try new things. He never lost weight though and within a year he was average for weight and this year he was in the seventieth percentile for both height and weight. Sure there are still days I worry about his eating habits or lack thereof as in just last night when I was told by the dorm staff at school he ate only two bites of chicken and a roll for dinner however at long last at the age of five we were able to say, adios, baby food!

Chapter 26

Things were continuing to go well for Jaden both at home and in school. Jaden was talking more and more now, and with that, some funny things were coming out of his mouth, as was the case in February 2012. It was a Monday night, and we were on the way back to school for swimming. Jaden kept asking me what sounded like, "Mom, you need ass?" I knew that he wasn't cursing at me, but I had no idea what he meant, and he would repeat this sentence a few times before finally saying, "Mom, your car is going low. Do you need ass?" Ahhh, the boy thought the car was going slowly, and he wanted to know if we needed *gas*. He was dropping the *g* and adding an *s*. I tried and tried to no avail to get him to pronounce the *g* sound. I'd have to send a note to school on that one, for I surely didn't ever want him going to school and saying something to the effect of Mom or Dad got ass last night. I could see the "oh my goodness what are they teaching this child at home" faces now. I'd also have to tell Gail, for she and Jaden would need to work on the *g* sound as well as other consonants.

There were other funny things that he was saying now, too, such as in March when I asked him what the best part of his day was. He paused and thought about it before replying, "Sitting next to pretty girls at lunch." Come to find out, he was sitting with the "big" girls in the K/1 class. It was nice to really start to see Jaden's true personality and to see his funny and witty side.

Spring had gone by rather uneventfully, and Jaden was continuing to make progress in all areas. Because the following school year Jaden would no longer be in pre-K, we now had to work with our local school district; New York Mills, as they, too, would get a say in Jaden's schooling. There was no doubt about it that Jaden was not ready for a mainstream school setting. He had matured so much in pre-K, but he still had so much maturing to do. I worried, would our local school district object to Jaden staying at NYSSD? After all, they did have Alex.

Alex is my friend Kristin's son, he is another deaf student who has excelled at New York Mills. Just last year he had a lead in the schools play—that's right, a deaf boy having a lead in a play in a mainstream school setting. When talking about deaf students succeeding in a mainstream school setting, Alex is the picture of success. Jaden and Alex, however, are very different. Alex has cochlear implants, Jaden does not. Jaden has to deal with the issues that 22q gives him, Alex does not. Alex's mom, Kristin, has had nothing but positive things to say about our home school district, and I myself know New York Mills is a great school, but in my heart I also knew that Jaden just wasn't ready yet.

Would our school district object to him staying at NYSSD? Were we now in for a fight to keep him in the school we wanted him to be in? The CSE chairperson called Cathy Lee and asked her several questions about Jaden: how much speech versus sign he uses, how he does academically, and so on. She even came to NYSSD to observe him in class. My stomach was in knots for weeks. Ultimately, the CSE was great to deal with. They had no objections to Jaden staying at NYSSD for kindergarten.

Summer was just around the corner, and the hurdle of determining where Jaden would go to school had been surmounted. Our next obstacle would now be to prepare Jaden for moving up to kindergarten. He was and is a boy who does not always like change, so at home we began hearing comments of "I not go to Theresa's class. I stay in Cathy Lee's class." Our goal was for the transition from pre-K to K to be a smooth one for us. Cathy, Gail, and I all talked to and prepared Jaden for moving into a new class, in hopes that it would be a smooth transition.

That summer was a hard time for our family. Glenn's dad, Ed—Jaden's papa—had become quite ill. Ed was a proud military man who would tell the stories of his navy days gone by to anyone willing to listen. He would share tales of how the President once slept on the ship he was working on, and of the great love of his life, his wife, Helen. As he got older, he sadly became quite ill with dementia and other health issues, and it was quite clear that he would not be with us much longer. Glenn's mom had passed away a few years prior, but Jaden was much younger then and hadn't grasped the concept. Jaden was older and more mature now; we'd need to begin preparing him for Papa's passing. We got books such as *The Fall of Freddie the Leaf* and *Sad Isn't Bad*. We talked about heaven, God, and angels. We brought Jaden to the hospital and to the nursing home to visit him and Jaden brought and delivered cards to him. On June 14, we said good-bye to

Papa. The following week would be the calling hours and funeral. Jaden handled Ed's passing relatively well. It helped that there were lots of end-of-school activities going on. Soon, there would be preparing for pre-K graduation and family camping trips and all sorts of other fun things going on to distract Jaden.

Jaden and his Papa

Chapter 27

Before we knew it, fall was here and Jaden would be headed off to kindergarten. Was Jaden ready to head off to the big-kid world of kindergarten and for all the new adventures that it would bring? Was I ready for it? Jaden was indeed ready for kindergarten, although he didn't think so.

Every single day for more than a month his mornings started off with tears and protests of "When I get to school I am going to Cathy's class! I am a little boy. I am not in kindergarten!" Morning, a time in the past I had always loved, for Jaden was often snuggly in the morning, became a time of dread and pure torture for both of us. "Yes," I would say, "you are going to Theresa's class! Yes, you are a big boy! Put your shoes on! If you don't stop now, you're going to your room after school!"

You would have thought we were throwing this kid to the wolves, but we weren't. NYSSD is a small school, a very small school, and with that there many are pros. A pro for Jaden was familiarity. Jaden would now be in a combined K/1 class with a teacher and teacher's aide, both of whom he was familiar with from summer school and other activities throughout the year. Two other boys who he knew from pre-K would be moving up to K with him, and he had been in pre-K for at least one year with the few kids moving from K to first grade. This should not have been so traumatic for him, and yet his world was crashing down around him.

Knock on wood, Jaden was saving all of his temper tantrums for home, as he never cried in school, never really tried to go next door to Cathy's class, was well behaved, and was doing really well in this new big boy world. I can't recall what is was, but one day a little over a month into school Jaden came home excited about something either that they had done in school that day or were going to be doing the next day, and suddenly that was it, the morning tears and temper tantrums had stopped. They were a thing of the past. At long last, we could go back to peaceful, snuggly mornings filled with my giving Jaden hugs, love, and back rubs.

I was very fortunate in that over the years I had developed what I feel was a great working relationship with Jaden's school team. As I've shared with the team members many times before, we could not have been blessed with a better group of instructors. Jaden truly has what I feel is the best partners on earth in his corner, an entire team of individuals working with him who possess the qualities and attributes that he needs most. Lord only knows how or why, but the kid hit the lottery, getting an entire support team of people like that.

The people behind Jaden have had to put up with one of the all-time neediest moms, year after year. Most teachers and staff will put up with a needy parent or one they don't mesh well with for one year, and that's it, but not this team. Jaden had been in pre-K for two and a half years and had been working with all but his physical therapist for just as long.

We were constantly talking, exchanging notes, e-mails, and phone calls, and more; the list goes on and on. My concerns were always graciously and kindly answered, never with a "Go away, Wendy," which I would've told myself years ago had I been in those professionals' shoes.

Jaden's entering kindergarten would be a transition for Mom, too. Would I mesh well with this new teacher? Would she be ready to deal with my kind of needy? My fingers were crossed that we would hit it off without a hitch. There would be homework, math, spelling, and more to be done on most nights. I would go from baking cakes for snack whenever I wanted, which was usually once a week, to an assigned snack day once a month, and as noted the snacks preferred would be healthy, with cakes and the like reserved for special occasions. Jeez, what would I do with all my free time now? My hobby for the past few years had been planning, baking, and decorating baked goods once a week. Yes, this new kindergarten world would be an adjustment on Mom, too.

Chapter 28

I didn't know it at the time, but Theresa ended up being exactly what we needed. I know that over the years other children and/or their parents have complained of homework being too long or hard or of the stricter structure of the K/1 classroom. Jaden was no exception. Getting used to having homework on a nightly basis was at first was a challenge for him, particularly if the homework was something he did not enjoy. Jaden didn't like things like coloring or writing. His fine motor skills remained weak, and in kindergarten coloring is often given for homework.

On those nights, there would often be tears at the kitchen table. Then there were other nights that homework would be something Jaden loved, like picking out an item for show and tell or getting to keep the class stuffed animal all week long and writing what the two of them did each night together. It took a while, but Jaden became used to this new big-kid kindergarten world.

When I heard complaints from other parents about there being too much homework in the K/1 class or about this or that not being liked, I always replied with something to the effect of "Knock on wood, we've always been very lucky and meshed very well with Theresa and have had no bumps in the road in dealing with her." I've reminded a few of the parents that she's got their kids' best interest at heart. I think it may be the whole transitioning from pre-K to K is an adjustment on all parents and children, and that Cathy and Theresa are both great teachers but they are also very different from each other.

The way I compare Cathy Lee to Theresa Matt is this. When a child is entering pre-K, it's a brand new world to the child and oftentimes the parents, too. The children often need to have their hand held and to be coddled a bit and Mom and Dad often times need the same. Cathy Lee does that. She gives parent and child the warm and fuzzies and makes pre-K a place they want to be. When a child is done with pre-K and ready for kindergarten, neither child nor parent needs their hand held as much. They need to be able to stand on their own two feet. They need to be challenged and to take on new challenges. They need to have structure, and for those kids who want to eventually attend a mainstream school setting, both parent and child need to start preparing for what that environment will be like. This is where Theresa comes into play. Theresa is a teacher who shows you what your kid is capable of, makes you study with them and do homework with them. Sure, it can be a pain at times, but this is what both parent and child need. School is still a fun learning environment; there's just always more work to be done.

Jaden and his K/1 teacher Theresa Matt

Chapter 29

As Jaden entered kindergarten, one area of concern for him was his social interaction with other students or lack thereof. It's not that Jaden didn't interact with students. It's just that he oftentimes preferred to be with the adults rather than the kids in a room. His class was small, and outside of class he didn't have a ton of interaction with other kids. We really needed to start boosting our efforts at home to give Jaden more interaction with other kids, so we decided that fall Jaden would start bowling.

James and Jen had been bowling for years and continued to bowl on Saturday mornings, so this would be a perfect start for Jaden. He seemed to like it. He had a bit of difficulty holding the bowling ball because it was a bit heavy for him, but he really liked rolling it toward the bowling pins. However, one of the reasons we were there was for him to interact with hearing peers in his age group, and though it's since changed, during his first year of bowling there just was not a ton of socialization going on. With encouragement from Glenn and me, Jaden would say hi to his playmates, but that was about it, in between his turns he would sit at the table or on my lap. We'd continue with bowling but would also eventually look into an additional activity for Jaden.

Jaden was off to a great year in kindergarten; he was excelling in reading and soon began doing spelling with the first graders. Theresa would work on things with Jaden that he didn't like doing, just to get him used to them and to help him overcome his disdain for particular activities. In class they did things like make Christopher Columbus projects that had, according to his teachers, "lots of folding, cutting. It was not easy for Jaden, but he soldiered through."

Perhaps it's because Jaden is hard of hearing and really fought hard for the speech that he has gained, but oftentimes his successes that I celebrate are speech related and that shouldn't really be the only successes I celebrate because his other triumphs, great and small, also deserve acknowledgment, too. This was so very evident in the gains he was making in his fine motor skills. Between being tag-teamed by his teacher and occupational therapist and working a lot on fine motor skills both in class and in therapy, his skills were bound to improve.

Jaden and Andrea had been working on snapping, fastening, and buttoning skills for quite some time. They used dressing toys, boards and his own clothing. On October 11, Jaden for the very first time was able to snap his own pants; this may seem small but was a huge success for Jaden. Stop to think about it. Jaden was five and a half years old, and every morning when he got dressed or every time he went to the bathroom he needed assistance in buttoning his pants. This one simple and small task had great impact on his independence, and he was finally able to do it. Yes indeed, this was a success to celebrate.

Chapter 30

In October another sad time for our family came. On October 27, just as I was getting Jaden ready for bed, the phone rang and it was one of my parents' neighbors. "Something has happened to your dad, and your mom needs you to come." I had never said more than a hello to my parents' neighbors, let alone gotten a phone call from them. I didn't know what was going on, but I knew it was serious.

Jaden and I headed over to my parents' house, and my mom was sitting on her front steps surrounded by neighbors. She looked at Jaden and said, "He has to go. You need to take him somewhere." I still didn't know what was going on, but I knew my father was in trouble. Glenn works right around the corner from my parents' house, so I took Jaden there. Not knowing all of the details, I explained to Jaden that Grandpa was sick and that he had to go to the hospital and the doctors were trying to help him. I told Glenn that I thought my dad might have died but wasn't sure and that I had to go, leaving Glenn to deal with Jaden and heading back to my parents' home.

I had only been gone about ten minutes, and by the time I got back police officers were there. My mom, who is a registered nurse, was saying through sobs that she had performed CPR but she didn't think it worked. A kind officer trying to give a glimmer of hope said he didn't know my dad's status but that the EMTs had intubated him before transport, which was a good sign.

We would soon be headed out the hospital, and I needed my mom to be prepared for what we would be walking into. I asked the officer to find out for me. He checked with someone and came back in and said my dad had passed. The sobs that erupted from my mom were one of the most painful sounds I've ever heard in my life. I went into the backyard and broke the news to my younger brother Dillon, then I called my older brother, Mike, in Florida. I asked if his partner, Katie, was home and he said yes and asked why. He knew right then and there that something was very, very wrong.

Glenn had dropped off Jaden at my sister and brother-in-law's house and had come over to my mom's. I let him know what was going on, and shortly thereafter the three of us left for the hospital. We spoke with the ER doctor, who said they worked on him for some time but their efforts proved fruitless. My dad, Michael, was a kind and gentle soul, usually mellow, and he was the biggest joke teller I have ever met. Man, he knew how to lay it on thick just for a laugh, which he was sure to get. My dad had many, many wonderful traits but he also had lifelong demons to deal with and he would eventually succumb to them. The cause of death was an accidental overdose on prescription pain medication. I've said many times that from my father I learned so much of who I do want to be and who I don't want to be. Some may take that statement as negative or disrespectful, but I meant it to be neither. I wouldn't trade any of the positive or negative experiences I had with my father for the world, for they have helped shape me into who I am today, and have taught me much about the parent I want to be for Jaden as well as the parent I never want to be for Jaden.

I would go back to my parents' home that night and stay the night. I had moved out in 2002. It was shortly after I told them about Glenn and I being together, and my leaving was not under the best of circumstances. This would be my first time spending the night there since then, and these certainly were not the circumstances I wanted to be back under. I made the appropriate phone calls, called the relatives that my mom wanted notified, and slept on her couch that night. The next day Carol and Bob would bring Jaden back home, he immediately ran to me and asked me how Grandpa was. I had notified everyone else, and now I need to tell Jaden that only four months after Papa had passed away, angels had come and taken Grandpa to heaven, too. It didn't seem fair to me that before he had reached the age of six he had been robbed of all but one grandparent. Jaden however was a trooper. He had been through it not too long ago, and sure there were tears but he handled this death quite well, too.

Jaden with his Grandpa and Grandma Keyes

Chapter 31

In November of 2012 Jaden was five years and nine months old and doing well, but his skills needed improvement in a few areas, one of which was his penmanship. Fine motor skills were still a particular weakness for Jaden, and the other area in need of improvement was all Moms' fault. Jaden needed to start working on not needing to be first all the time.

A few notes came home saying that he got upset when he wasn't first or that he had left his belongings in school because he was "_very_ preoccupied with rushing to be first in line." My thought? *Oh crap! This is my fault!* Jaden tends to be a dawdler, so at home every night we had been playing a "racing game" that I'd made up to race Jaden to see who could get ready for bed and then reach Jaden's bed first. While doing the dishes or something else, I would say "I bet you can't be ready before I am done!" The game worked, too. His taking forever and a day to get his pajamas on and pick out a bedtime story was sped up times ten.

I didn't think this silly made-up game would have repercussions and negative impacts in other areas, I quickly put the kibosh on that game and had several talks with Jaden about slowing down, and you don't always have to be first, etc. However, he did have issues with this for quite some time including in February 2013 when a note came home saying he had had a few pushing episodes while trying to be first and that "he seems overly focused on being first, or getting the first pick of anything . . ." *Crap, with one little game and I've damaged my kid for life!*

I had to fess up and tell the teacher that some of these behaviors were my fault—and about our who-can-be-first game. We really had to focus on that and this would be a reoccurring theme throughout the remainder of the school year, one that we even discussed with Cindy, the school psychologist. Today I'm happy to report that it seems I didn't really damage my kid for life, as he is no longer overly focused on being first.

Another issue in November of 2012 was Jaden being rude. There were a few instances in which he touched other people's belongings or told them the way in which they were placed were wrong. First was his desire to always be first, and then there was this.

Theresa was absent one day in November and there was a substitute teacher. Jaden had become accustomed to nightly homework and there was no homework being given that day. Jaden tends to be routine oriented and so he was upset by this and quite rudely he actually told the substitute that she was doing her job wrong and she was supposed to give homework! Jaden had made such a big stink about there being no homework and it was the very next day that he was in such a rush to first in line that he somehow forgot his book-bag at school and therefore was not able to complete his homework that night!

Visions of stories that began like this ran through my head "Once upon a time there was a nice little boy named Jaden. Jaden then turned into an evil brat monster. The End" I surly did not want my child being known as the brat in school. I wanted my sweet little boy back. In addition to having discussions about not always needing to be first we now have to have discussions with Jaden about not being rude, we would explain that different teachers do things differently and that this is okay. We would also have to talk to him about not touching items that belong to another person. His teacher would reach out to the school psychologist for her input and she would remind me that "it's the actions, not the boy, that are troubling."

Chapter 32

The winter holidays had passed and January had arrived. The hot topic in January 2013 was "Do you feed your child?" A note had come home from Theresa:

We were having a discussion about what we ate for lunch and healthy food choices. Kids told what fruit or vegetable they also had with lunch. Then we talked about what we might want to eat for dinner tonight. Jaden couldn't or wouldn't tell one thing he wanted for dinner or what he had for dinner last night. So, we gave him choices to jog his memory—but still nothing! So Gail and I are wondering what he eats at home for dinner or what foods he prefers now . . . ?

Oh my gosh, they think I don't feed my kid . . . I replied back with the following:

95% of the time he has veggies, carrots & broccoli are his favorite . . . then usually a meat of some kind (hot dog, chicken, or turkey) he won't eat ham, pork, hamburger, noodles, or pizza . . . We really do feed him. He's still a picky eater, but at least it's not baby food, which he ate for forever . . .

Theresa replied,

Ha ha! I had no doubt that you feed him, but was having a difficult time getting him to share with the group dinner foods he has with the family . . .

Phew! I thought. *They know I do feed my child!*

Chapter 33

Jaden turned six in February 2013 and was doing well in all areas, but the common consensus was that he needed more interaction with other kids aside from the kids he knew at school and from bowling on Saturdays, where his interaction with others was limited. The hunt was on to get him involved in something else, and ultimately we decided to give gymnastics a go.

He really enjoyed it, and within a month his physical therapist was noticing improvements during PT, particularly on the balance beam, which Jaden had been working on. I must admit, and I'd be a liar if I failed to say, that it was and still is often hard for me to watch him during gymnastics. Jaden does not lack motivation and gives it his all, but to watch him week after week struggle to do activities that seem to come with relative ease to the other boys in his class is somewhat painful for me to watch. Nonetheless, he always says he enjoys it and seems to be having fun.

In March, Jaden's class did a unit on animals, complete with a trip to the pet store, my child fell in love with the rodent, specifically the guinea pigs. He drew pictures of them and picked out names for them. He tried to convince his teacher that the class pet should be a hamster or guinea pig, and when they choose a fish he began asking weekly if he could have a guinea pig at home. My answer was always the same. "No, we are not getting a guinea pig." This lasted for months and months until we finally caved and bought him one the following year for his seventh birthday.

In the spring, just as in all the years before, decision time had come again. Would Jaden stay at NYSSD for first grade, or would we enroll him in the local elementary school? The decision this year would be another easy one for me. If Jaden was to stay, he would still be in the Little Listeners program, and he would have Theresa as his teacher again. We loved the program, and we loved the teacher, so it was a no-brainer, and of course we wanted him to stay.

The year before, I had become familiar with the process of how the MDT/IEP Multidisciplinary Team (MDT) Individual Education Program (IEP) meeting would go, and so though I still had a knot or two in my stomach I was much less concerned about our local school district having issues with Jaden staying at NYSSD. Just as it had the year prior, the meeting went well, and it was determined that Jaden was free to stay at NYSSD.

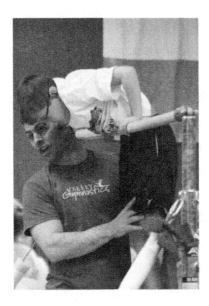

Jaden giving it his all during gymnastics

Chapter 34

One longtime area of concern for Jaden that I have yet to mention, were our early concerns about Jaden's vision. Dating from the time Jaden started school around age three in 2010, Andrea, his occupational therapist, had had concerns that he was not focusing correctly or that he perhaps had visual perception issues. Cathy Lee, his pre-K teacher, and later Theresa Matt, his kindergarten teacher, also had similar concerns.

Lately, when reading, Jaden would often lean his head close to the page with his right eye close to the table, so that he appeared to be focusing on the words with his left eye. The concern was if that if he had visual problems, then that could be affecting his fine and gross motor skills. Visual issues, we realized, might help to explain his weak penmanship skills and might even help to explain his difficulties with balance.

There were too many e-mails to count back and forth between Andrea and me regarding suspected visual issues, and during that time Jaden had multiple vision exams, but the ophthalmologist always gave him the all clear, though due to his medical history and other issues we even met with a neuro-ophthalmologist, but she, too, gave Jaden the all clear. I believed those working with Jaden, but if the doctors were giving his vision a clean bill of health, what was I to do? Finally, in April of 2013, we were told Jaden needs glasses. Not all but some of the visual issues seemed to improve once he finally had glasses. Jaden was not squinting to see the paper as much and appeared to have an easier time focusing; overall he did quite well adjusting to the glasses.

That spring Jaden's physical and social skills had improved by leaps and bounds, with many thanks to Theresa. Jaden's food choices were still somewhat limited, so Theresa had decided to do a food unit that would of course benefit all of the kids but especially Jaden. The kids were trying all sorts of things such as Sour Patch Kids, pineapple, and much more. The class was doing projects such as making potato chips with sea salt and more. The kids made grids keeping track of what they tried, what the texture and taste of the items were, what each child thought of the item, etc. Sure there were many things Jaden did not like, but that wasn't the point; he was trying them! No fuss, no tears, no meltdowns. Theresa had this boy trying things such as chicken salad sandwich, kiwi, and coconut. These are things that in a million years he never would have tried before, and his food choices have only continued to improve since then.

Chapter 35

Summer would bring one of my favorite moments of 2013. We had switched audiologists again. The team we were seeing in Syracuse was great, but if possible we wanted to have someone closer to home. Kim, Jaden's school audiologist, would put us in touch with another Kim. When Jaden was younger, he had seen Kim Keane one other time, shortly after we stopped going to our local hospital and before we were seeing the group in Syracuse. We decided to make the switch to Kim Keane, and we love her!

One of the first things Kim would do was turn up Jaden's hearing aid, the volume of which had not been adjusted in years, since Kim had first seen him in 2009. Unbeknownst to me Jaden was ready for and needed a big boost. The June day that Kim adjusted his hearing aid, I was doing dishes in the kitchen and Jaden told me he heard a sound in his room. I more or less blew it off, saying, "Oh, Jaden, I'm sure it's nothing," and went about my business.

A few days later, Jaden heard the sound again. He took me by the hand and said, "You have to hear this. It's back. I think there is a monster in my room." Poor kid! It took me a minute to figure out what Jaden was hearing. The light in his room was set up so that when he turned on the light, the ceiling fan would also come on. He was hearing the oscillation of the ceiling fan. The fan was not new to Jaden; it was something that had been on hundreds if not thousands of times before, and yet there was a true look of confusion and fear in his eyes.

Jaden had been exposed to this sound since birth and apparently had not noticed or been able to hear it before June of 2013. I had never really thought about Jaden hearing or not hearing something as simple as a ceiling fan before. I just assumed he was hearing it and knew what the sound was. It was one of those moments that make you really take notice and realize the everyday sounds that we hear and take for granted that someone like Jaden, who has a hearing impairment, may be missing out on.

Chapter 36

Jaden did gymnastics throughout the spring, but we had decided to take a break during the summer sessions, and in August before signing him back on for the fall, rather than encourage Jaden, I discouraged him.

"Maybe we should try something different, because sometimes you have a hard time keeping up with the boys and need lots of help from the coach. What do you think?"

He replied with more wisdom than I had. "That's okay, Mommy. Someday I can do flips like the other boys. I just have to try lots. I want to do gymnastics."

So gymnastics was a go. We were signing him up again for the fall. Yes, my wise boy, you keep trying. An A plus for you and an F minus "mom fail" for me. No, I did not like to see Jaden struggle week after week, and I still wish that we could find his niche—try other things, but find the one thing he really excels at—but on that day I learned from a six-year-old boy to study his face. Does his face reflect sadness and defeat, or is his the face of a child who is struggling yet determined? If it's the latter of the two—which thus far it always has been—then who am I to discourage rather than encourage him? If he is not bothered by the fact that he cannot do something, and he enjoys making the attempt, then why should it bother me? The short answer is, it shouldn't and it doesn't, and when the other boys have been doing a certain activity for weeks on end and Jaden finally gets it, finally succeeds, then watching the look of satisfaction and pride on his face is so well worth it. I'll admit, it is enough to bring tears to my eyes in a packed gym.

Summer had quickly passed, and now, in the fall of 2013 at age six and a half, Jaden would be entering first grade. His school year started off well. The school audiologist, Kim, had been eating lunch with the kids, and she made it her mission to get Jaden to try even more new foods. He finally caved and tried both a grilled cheese sandwich and tomato soup for her. He didn't like the soup, but grilled cheese sandwiches became one of his favorites. Jaden was still getting all of his therapies, and in class Theresa was still working on things to benefit Jaden as well. In mid-October they read the book *The Ugly Duckling* and acted it out. As Theresa reported,

> Jaden was not thrilled walking like a duck. It was hard for him but he did his best (squatting on feet—he kept wanting to kneel—and waddling). Then we did some crossover exercises (ex. Touch your right "wing" to your left knee—crossing midline). As you know he has difficulty with these, that's why we practice, but he avoids these types of things (Jaden: "I think it's time for my speech!").

Nothing too significant was going on with Jaden. He did start dance classes at school that fall and really seemed to enjoy those. He had run-of-the-mill spelling and math tests and related work. He would work on using inventive spelling as opposed to always needing to know how to spell something. Jaden would learn that it's okay to sound a word out, and that if it's not perfect, that is fine. This would drive him crazy, at times he can be a bit of a perfectionist, and the thought of not spelling something correctly bothered him terribly.

Chapter 37

Late that fall of Jaden's first grade year, I entered his photo into a calendar contest for the International 22q11.2 Foundations yearly Faces of Sunshine calendar. He was chosen as the face of June.

In December, there were concerns that Jaden was missing some sounds (*f, th, sh*), as his speech was not as good, or clear, as it had been. In class, he was having trouble focusing on the speaker or sometimes even finding the speaker. Kim at school would call Kim Keane so that those issues could be addressed at his hearing appointment in December.

Jaden's hearing hadn't seemed to change much in the six months since he'd had his last hearing evaluation, and so we weren't sure what was up with the decline in his speech. Even though we didn't really get the answer as to why there had been a decline in Jaden's speech, it still turned out to be a very exciting appointment.

A new pediatric hearing aid had recently come out, and we decided to proceed with ordering it for Jaden. He hadn't gotten a new hearing aid since his first ones in 2009, and the technology keeps changing and improving, and so he was long overdue and ready for a new one. This new hearing aid would, hopefully, allow Jaden to hear higher-frequency sounds that he had not been hearing before, or at least not consistently, such as *s*-sounds, it was also said to be more water resistant. And as a plus for Jaden, they now came in neat colors, and so he was able to pick the color he wanted. The new hearing aid was ordered, and he would get it the first week of January.

In January 2014, things were busy in the Roback house. Glenn would be having surgery for a knee injury and Jaden would be getting his new hearing aid. We picked up Jaden's new aid on the third. Jaden would comment that he liked it and it sounded different, but he couldn't articulate what it was that he liked or that sounded different about it. We didn't notice any improvements in Jaden's speech, but he was hearing more environmental sounds. For example, shortly after getting his hearing aid, the washer was running and the water was draining from it, Jaden asked what that sound was. This was a new sound to him that he had not previously heard. We were happy to have better technology and to have this new aid for Jaden.

Chapter 38

Have you ever had a moment where you wish you were someone else, even if just for a moment? That was me from January to April of 2014. Our family had been going through the great big debate of to mainstream or not to mainstream for Jaden's next year of school. Okay, in all fairness I guess I shouldn't say it was a great big debate for our family. Really it was just for my husband and me, as everyone else said they didn't know and wouldn't want to have to choose. And my husband and I, well, we were on the same team. So I guess it was really Wendy's GREAT BIG debate (all within her own little head).

I've been very fortunate in that I've always felt confident in and never doubted our educational decisions for Jaden. First, we had decided he needed EI, though some didn't agree it was the necessary course at the time. I thought Jaden needed it, and so we pursed it. As I've said, our home soon became a revolving door of therapists: physical, speech and occupational therapy, basic skills and a teacher of the deaf. I never doubted that.

Our next decision had been when to put Jaden in pre-K. The options were to wait until he was three and a half, or to start him when he was so little, not even three and still wobbly on his feet. He needed the interaction with kids, so even though he was wobbly on his feet, we sent him on his way. I never doubted that decision.

From there we'd had to decide where to send him He could go to a regular pre-K to be with hearing kids his age, or he could go to the school for the deaf. I asked myself, *If he's with other deaf kids who, like him, don't talk, how will he ever learn to talk?* No, no, no . . . The idea was for Jaden to get the teaching and support that he needed. We liked the teacher, the class, and the speech therapist. Jaden would go the school for deaf. I never doubted that decision either.

NYSSD is a small school, and one of the many positives to this is that you see the same moms year after year and you develop acquaintances with them. You feel comfortable making small talk and asking questions of each other, such as, "Have you made any decisions?"

At this time, however, being asked the above question would lead me to wish I were someone else, specifically any one of the other moms. For they seemed to have all figured out, and I surely didn't.

The mom of one of the children has always said of her child, "I'm never going to mainstream him. He will forever stay at this school. Kids are mean, and he does not need to experience how mean they can be." Another mom said her child would stay at NYSSD because "we tried mainstreaming with her brother and it didn't work out, so she'll be staying." Another mom I put the question to said, "We'll be mainstreaming him. We've had some bumps in the road here, and so we'll mainstream him, if not this year, then the year after." And then you ask one other mom and she seems to be torn just like you, but then she says, "I think we're leaning toward mainstreaming. We think he'll have better real-life experience in a mainstream setting."

So there I was staring at these moms, and thinking, *How the heck do you have it all figured out? Why can't I be like you? You see, if we'd always said we will or we won't, we wouldn't have to be dealing with this now. But no, us Robacks, we're the difficult family, the family that always says we'll evaluate on a year-by-year basis to determine whatever is best for our child. And now the time has come to make a decision, and I don't know what to choose.* I made lists of pros and cons, and I asked those whose opinions matter to me to look at the lists and tell me what their choice would be, that is, if they were in my shoes, and—gulp—I still didn't have an answer.

So what does one do? Well, if you're me, you take a shower to wash away the stresses of the day, and while in the shower you do what every logical mom in this predicament would do: you play eenie, meenie, miney, mo in the shower with loofah sponges that just happen to be in the school colors of each of your choices. You wait. Wait for the light bulb to go off, for that aha moment but realize all too soon that you won't get it by playing eenie meenie miney mo in the shower, so you rinse the shampoo off your hair, finish your shower, and continue to get ready for bed.

So now you're left wishing that, if only for a moment, you were one of the other moms, one of the ones who knows the right choice. You throw your PJs on and head to bed, knowing that tomorrow is another day, knowing that many moms have been in this position before you and there will be many more there after you. You go to bed knowing that the team behind you will help ensure that you make the right choice. Knowing that when the time comes to finally make the choice, it will be the right one— and that if you really need to, you can always toss a coin, seeing as eenie, meenie, miney, mo didn't work out so well.

This was how I felt for months. You see, this was the very first year after sending him to NYSSD that I was unsure as to which placement would be best for Jaden. The decision-making process began in early January, and it wasn't until early April that I would finally make a decision.

The reason Glenn and I were under pressure to make a decision about Jaden's next year is that the Little Listeners program that he had been enrolled in since pre-K only goes through first grade. Second through twelfth graders at NYSSD enter the school's total communication program, in which some children sign and some children use sign and voice. Jaden would continue to get speech therapy, but the focus would no longer be on listening, language, and speech acquisition skills, as it had been all of the years prior. This is what made for such a very tough decision for us. We loved the Little Listeners program and felt the program meshed the deaf and hearing worlds perfectly for Jaden, giving him the best of both. I wholeheartedly wished this program continued through twelfth grade, since if it did my decision would have been easy. But since it doesn't, this was the first time I would doubt my ability to make a sound and accurate decision for Jaden.

Glenn would give me his input, but ultimately he would leave the choice to me. I would ask Theresa, Gail, Kim, Andrea, and Cindy for their thoughts and input; and Glenn would ask Tom,

Jaden's current physical therapist, what he thought. As I knew they would, each person we asked gave Glenn and me their open and honest opinions, which is what we needed and wanted, but their opinions on the topic were just as diverse as were Glenn's and mine, and so it didn't really help narrow the choice down.

This was the first time that part of me felt Jaden was ready to mainstream, but another part of me still had so many doubts and concerns about attempting such a transition. With each and every pro, there was also a con. NYSSD had small classes. Pro: lots of one-on-one instruction and support. Con: not a lot of or a wide variety of social interaction. On the flip side, New York Mills had larger class sizes. Pro: lots of social interaction and stimulation. Con: it would be much harder for Jaden to get caught up when he leaves class for his therapies. My list making of pros and cons would go on and on, and I was not sure as to what made the scale tip more one way or the other. Glenn felt from the get-go that Jaden should continue at NYSSD. I would flip-flop back and forth, one day feeling New York Mills was the way to go, and the very next day feeling NYSSD was the right place for Jaden for the next year.

I would have nightmare after nightmare about the decision that needed to be made. One night I would dream that Jaden stayed at NYSSD but that academically his work had declined due to his not be challenged enough, and the next night I would dream that we put him in New York Mills and that he hated it and started to revert back to the old Jaden; shy and more quirky. The nightmares would be long and vivid. When I finally did make a decision, I only did so out of frustration, hoping there would be no more nightmares.

Glenn, Theresa, Gail, and I would go to New York Mills to meet with the second grade teachers. Later, Gail, Jaden, and I would go to New York Mills so that he could visit the school and a class. Glenn and I would go back to New York Mills to ask follow-up questions, and Glenn and I would also visit NYSSD's second grade class to get a feel for that, too.

I knew from talking with several people that if we were going to mainstream Jaden, this was the year to do it. I'd also heard from many people that the two second grade teachers at New York Mills were awesome and would be the perfect teachers to introduce Jaden to a mainstream school setting, and one of the two teachers had taught the aforementioned Alex and so had some familiarity in working with deaf or hard of hearing kids. After several meetings at both schools, I was still unbelievably torn, because it seemed neither setting was the perfect setting for Jaden at the time.

April came, and it was time to finally make a decision. In a few short weeks, we would be having Jaden's IEP meeting and a decision needed to be made prior to that. I realized that when I weighed all of the concerns I had, both by number and the severity of the concern, that I had more concerns and more severe concerns about putting Jaden in New York Mills than I did about keeping him at NYSSD. Yet my gut said, "Give it a go, Try NYM, and if it doesn't work, put Jaden back in NYSSD."

Glenn's gut, however, said the opposite. It told Glenn that he was not opposed to mainstreaming Jaden, but he didn't think this next year was the year to do it. His gut said, "Jaden's done so well at NYSSD, he's happy there, he gets speech therapy daily from a therapist who's familiar with him, and with working with deaf/ HOH kids he should continue to stay there at least for next year."

Because I was the indecisive one, and the one who had been flip-flopping back and forth with regard to my feelings, and Glenn had been decisive from the get-go and felt from the go that Jaden should stay at NYSSD next year, his gut won. We decided to stick with NYSSD for second grade.

Who can say if I made the right choice or the wrong choice. As Cindy said to me, "Because both options carry pros and cons, that means that there IS no definite right or wrong choice, and therefore no big mistake to fear making!" This is the choice we made, and now we were able to move forward with prepping for next year. I had knots in my stomach when e-mailing Jaden's team to tell them our decision, for I knew some of them leaned much more toward mainstreaming. Would they think I was setting my kid up for failure? They were all very supportive of the decision we made, and hopefully when fall comes and Jaden starts second grade he'll continue to thrive and excel.

We'll see how things go for Jaden this upcoming school year, and then as we've done each year so far we'll reevaluate and decide which placement is best for Jaden for third grade. Hopefully it won't be such a touch decision, and the choice will come easily to me, but if it doesn't I'm prepared to make lists of pros and cons again and to look to Jaden's team again for their thoughts, input, and support just as I've always done.

Chapter 39

It may seem as if during the first part of 2014 our time was fully and totally occupied with making the decision as to what placement was best for Jaden, and in truth a lot of my time was focused on that. However, the beat goes on, and there were several other things happening.

In January, we would send Jaden's bike to school, and he and his physical therapist, Tom, would begin to work on balancing on the bike without training wheels. Jaden was not happy about this at all and had more than one meltdown over it "I can't do it! I can't do it! If I was a bigger boy I would sneak my training wheels to school and put them back on all by myself!" He's not mastered it yet. Actually, he's not even close, and at home Jaden still uses a bike with training wheels, but Tom hasn't given up on Jaden and they are still working on it. I'm confident that, with Jaden's determination and Tom's help, Jaden will indeed one day soon master this skill.

February and March would go by without anything major going on. Jaden turned seven and, as I've noted, at long last got the guinea pig he had been asking for since the class visit to a pet store a year prior.

April, however, well, there was a bit more going on. Glenn would have a total knee replacement, and then from there he would go to inpatient physical rehabilitation for several weeks. In between swimming on Monday nights and gymnastics on Tuesday nights, Jaden and I visited Glenn at the rehab center most days. It made for a busy a month.

One concern with Jaden staying at NYSSD is making sure he gets enough interaction with hearing peers his age. I think and hope we do okay on that front. He'll continue to do bowling and gymnastics in the fall, and in April we also decided to give AYSO soccer a try. Jaden enjoyed that, and so he'll play again in the fall. Soccer is not something that comes of particular ease to Jaden, but when watching him on the field you can see the focus in his eyes as he's watching his surroundings and getting instruction. Then there are the times where he's not so focused, such as one day when, mid-practice, he stopped, pointed, and shouted, "Hey, Mom look at the pretty butterfly" just as the ball was coming to him and he should have been kicking it. It was quite comical to the other parents there. Overall, for his first time playing soccer, he did well. At some point in the future, I'm sure Glen and I will continue to look into more activities for Jaden.

May would come and so would my thirtieth birthday. The day before my birthday, I was finally able to fulfill a lifelong dream of skydiving. Several people thought I was nuts, but it was great. I would do it again in a heartbeat.

On the actual day of my birthday, we celebrated at an event called 22q At The Zoo. The event was held at the zoo in Syracuse, and it commemorates 22q Worldwide Awareness Day, an event that brings families together that are affected by 22q. We had gone in 2013 for the first time and had really enjoyed ourselves. The event was great this year as well! There were crafts, caricature drawings, a performance by a bubble performer, lunch, and then of course exploring the zoo. Theresa came this year, too. Jaden was thrilled about that. It was a wonderful event, and fun was had by all.

In June, there would again be concerns about Jaden's vision. He goes to the ophthalmologist every six months, and it had only been four months since his last visit, but we had become worried that his vision had changed again. In class, he was again leaning close to the paper and focusing with only one eye. So we brought him back to the ophthalmologist, from whom we learned that his vision had indeed changed quite a bit in only four months. The doctor explained that it's not uncommon to see significant changes in such a short time period when the child has a predisposition for nearsightedness such as Jaden does. He said we could expect to see Jaden's vision continue to worsen until he is done growing, with more rapid deterioration happening when Jaden is going through or is about to go through a growth spurt. Unfortunately nothing can really be done to prevent or lessen that.

As for our long-standing concerns with Jaden's habit of focusing with one eye, we also finally got information on that, as his ophthalmologist had likewise picked up on the mannerism at this visit. We were told that one of Jaden's eyes is aligned slightly higher than the other; therefore, Jaden is picking and choosing an eye to focus with versus using them both together at the same time. He said Jaden will likely always do this, though he has no significant lazy eye and because, independently of each other, both eyes are functioning as they should, there isn't really anything that needs to be done or can be done for this either. Finally Andrea's very long-standing concerns about Jaden having focusing issues had been validated. Andrea had retired in the fall, but I had to e-mail her to provide her with this Jaden update.

Chapter 40

Jaden with his pet Rocket

That brings us to today. Jaden just finished first grade and will be starting summer school next week. He is a boy who brings me laughter daily and never ceases to amaze me. It was just about two weeks ago that he couldn't wait to get home from swimming. He didn't say anything in the car on the way home, but once we arrived home he couldn't get in the door quick enough to show me his new skill. Jaden had finally learned to tie his shoe, which was a skill he had been working on in occupational therapy for over two years. He was extremely proud of himself, as he should have been, and just this past weekend he asked to take a frog-catching class while at camp. That's right, my once-upon-a-time squeamish boy was looking forward to catching and touching frogs, and several of them at that. Jaden is full of surprises and continues to thrive and meet the challenges thrown his way.

When I think of Jaden, his story, and what it is and what it means, I think two things, one being the saying "knowledge is power" is so very true. Accept the knowledge that others can give you about your child; embrace it and use it to help your child. Don't be ashamed or embarrassed to admit when you don't know something. Instead, use your resources and the networks you develop to help you gain the knowledge you seek. Use any and all aids to guide you through your journey. For our family, it is the knowledge that we have been given about Jaden, both good and not so good, that has allowed us to help him become the wonderful little boy he is today. The other thing I think of when I think of what Jaden's story is that having a special needs child is not as life shattering as some may believe. It may not be the life you had envisioned rather it may actually end up being much better than anything you could have ever envisioned.

Chapter 41

Glenn, Jaden and myself

What I know from raising Jaden thus far:

I do know that I don't know what the future holds for Jaden, just as none of us knows what the future holds for any of our children.

I do know that there will be bumps and bruises along the way, as is typical for all children. Perhaps Jaden will have different, and maybe more, challenges due to 22q and his hearing loss, but we'll leave it to God for now and address those issues as they arise.

I do know that whatever curves life throws at Jaden, if we take things one day at a time we can handle them as a family and help Jaden overcome any obstacles that he needs to overcome.

I do know that Jaden has a determination that not many children his age have, and through his own hard work, motivation, and eagerness he's already met many of the obstacles thrown his way and I am confident he will continue to do so.

I do know that I've met many awesome people, quite a few of whom I am fortunate enough to now call friends who, if it were not for Jaden, I would likely never have crossed paths with.

I do know that 22q and deafness are parts of Jaden, they are parts of him that are meant to be acknowledged and embraced, not denied or hidden.

I do know that though 22q and deafness are parts of Jaden, they are not the sum of his parts but rather are a small thread in the fabric that is Jaden; 22q and deafness do not, will not, and should not define him. There is so much more to who Jaden is than 22q and being deaf.

I do know that like all little boys, Jaden loves to play and loves to have fun, is smart, witty, silly, has a love of learning and reading, is sometimes naughty, and is always loving and always loveable.

I do know that if today I were given the chance to have a "normal" child instead of Jaden, I would say nay. If he wasn't deaf and if he didn't have 22q, chances are we would have a much different little boy. Jaden is perfect just the way he is.

I do know that if given the chance to do it all over again I would, in a heartbeat. It's been a wild ride so far, filled with highs and lows, but it's certainly a ride I never want to get off of. I look forward to watching the future unfold for Jaden and seeing what it entails for us.

Cindy once told me that she refers to Jaden as "Vitamin J" and that "a daily dose of Vitamin J does a person good". I think this sentiment fits Jaden perfectly as one last thing I know because of Jaden is that I am a better me because of him. Much of the person I am and have become is because of Jaden. Actually, I know that most people whose lives Jaden has touched have been left better off than they were before meeting him, our wonderful child, our Vitamin J.

The Roback Family

Acknowledgments

First and foremost, thank you to God, with whom all things are possible.

To Jaden, thank you for being the awesome little boy that you are. Thank you for bringing love, laughter, and amazement to my life on a daily basis. I love you to the moon, the stars, all of the planets, and back.

To Glenn, thank you for being the wonderful father that you are to the kids, and for being there for me these past dozen-plus years. I love you!

To James and Jen, I know it's not always been easy being an older sibling to a child so much younger than you, but thanks for always putting up with your brother, letting him know he's loved, and for being there for him. I love you both more than words can ever say.

To my mother, Dorothy Keyes, thank you for giving me life. Thank you for always being there for me and our family. I couldn't do this thing called life without you. I love you!

To my brother Michael Keyes Jr.; his partner, Katie McDermot; and their kids Emilee, Michael, and Cameron. Thank you for being an involved and loving part of Jaden's story, even though it is from a distance. I only wish we lived closer together so that Jaden could grow up seeing his cousins even more often.

To my younger brother Dillon Tyler Keyes, I love you! If you keep your head on straight, we know you can and will have a bright future ahead of you.

To my Uncle Pat and Aunt Barb, thank you for being a huge part of my story. Thank you for always being there for me. I love you both!

To my Roback family, Kathy, Linda, Bone, Cira, and family, thank you for being a huge part of Jaden's story and for always being there for him.

To my Synakowski family, Carol, Bob, Melissa, Josh, Kristen, Reagan, and Eli, Jaden is a very lucky little boy to have all of you in his corner. Such a large part of his story surrounds all of you. As for me, you are another bunch who I couldn't do this crazy thing called life without. Family by marriage; friends by choice. I love each of you. When I married Glenn, I married his family, and I am so lucky to have each of you in my life not only as family but as my friends.

To the Caban, Oliver, Dolan family, everyone needs to have someone who makes them feel grounded and connected to their roots. Far or near, you are that family for me and have been since I was a nine-year-old little girl. I am blessed that you continue to be a part of my life and that we have reconnected over the years. Thank you! XoXo!

To my other besties, Amanda Gehrke, Hilary Webb, and Heather Entwistle. I don't get together with any of you near enough, but thank you for always being there for me. Thank you for being huge parts of my story!

To Jaden's pediatrician, Dawn Bard, M.D., and the entire staff at Utica Pediatrics, thanks for keeping my boy healthy and for keeping his mama sane.

To Jaden's audiologists, his two Kims, Kimberly Sacco and Kimberly Keane, we could not ask for better audiologists for Jaden. My boy loves you both! Thank you for helping and guiding our family. Thank you for putting up with this crazy, needy mama and answering any and all of the countless random questions that I've had.

To Jaden's early intervention team at Children's Therapy Network, Lauren Hurlbut, Lisa Dite, Mike Wilkosz, and Anne Nelson, thank you for being part of Jaden's story early on. Thank you for helping to put Jaden on the path to becoming the awesome boy that he is today.

To Joan Fargnoli, I will never ever be able to adequately thank you! Thank you for being a part of Jaden's early story. Thank you for helping not only Jaden but our entire family during the early years. You were indeed a godsend to us when we were first navigating the world of having a deaf/HOH child, and we would not have come through intact if it were not for you. I am beyond blessed to be able to call you a friend. XoXo!

To the Little Listeners teachers, Cathy Lee, Theresa Matt, and to the teachers assistants who you have had over the years, including Nancy Lopus, Kathy Morreale, Nancy Richards, and Mary Ann McVicar, thank you for being a *huge* part of Jaden's current story. Cathy and Theresa (and your assistants), there is no doubt in my mind that Jaden would not be the boy that he is today if it were not for your love, time, effort, and guidance! You have helped to develop Jaden into an awesome being.

To Jaden's therapy team, Gail Ashmore, Andrea Rounds, Kelly Cohen, and Tom Sunderlin, thank you for helping Jaden reach goals that once upon a time we never even would have envisioned for him.

To everyone else at NYSSD who has worked and interacted with Jaden, thank you! There are far too many of you to mention here, but know that you, too, have been a *huge* part of Jaden's story. Thank you for positively influencing and impacting the life of my child. I can truly say Jaden loves NYSSD, all of the friends he has made there, and all of the staff who have worked with him.

To Kristin Hubley, thank you for being the first parent of a deaf child to reach out to me. Thank you for continuing to check in on us from time to time and being a part of our story. Your reaching out to us was and continues to be much appreciated.

And, finally, a special thank-you to Murleen Oliver and Gail Ashmore. You ladies were the first two individuals to plant the seed in my head that I should perhaps think of penning a book. You both happened to make that suggestion around the same time, and this book likely would have never been started had it not been for your promptings. Thank you both for that! I am blessed and fortunate to be able to call both of you ladies my friends!

For anyone who I may have forgotten to mention who has had a positive impact on myself or Jaden, THANK YOU! I know there are many others who I have failed to thank here, but do please know you are appreciated.